Clackmannan
— AND THE OCHILS —

INCLUDED in the district coat of arms are the immortal words, *Look about ye.* We should not ignore this advice, for there are treasures to be found throughout Clackmannanshire.

This illustrated guide comprehensively records the wealth of our architectural heritage and allows the reader to reflect on the way in which the built environment has responded over the centuries to the ever-changing demands of society.

Buildings, constructed with care and pride, fill these pages. With growing confidence, our contemporary society can and must continue these fine traditions for future generations.

The support of Clackmannan District Council for this publication is greatly appreciated.

DUNCAN C. STIRLING
PRESIDENT
The Stirling Society of Architects

Author: Adam Swan
Series Editor: Charles McKean
© Adam Swan and RIAS

Scottish Academic Press
Royal Incorporation of Architects in Scotland
ISBN 07073 0513 6
1st edition 1987
Printed by Lindsay & Co. Ltd., Edinburgh

INTRODUCTION

Clackmannanshire, Scotland in epitome and historically her smallest county, occupies a tiny portion of central Scotland on the north banks of the river Forth, populated by under 50,000 persons. Her boundaries are Stirling's huge Abbey Craig rock to the west, the impressive Ochil hills to the north, and Kinross and Fife to the east. The hills and the great river provided barriers which ensured Clackmannanshire's seclusion: the most vital battles in Scots history were fought on her very doorstep, whilst she offered peaceful retreats to her country's leaders.

An exceptional series of tower houses were occupied by the Bruce, Erskine, Argyll and Schaw families, attendants on the Stewart monarchs at their favoured seat of Stirling. Yet this tiny territory contained other towers and castles as well — Hartshaw, Alva, Manor, Menstrie, Tillicoultry, the Blair, Glendevon, and the Bishop's Palace at Cowden; all but three now vanished. Clackmannanshire lairds were amongst the first in Scotland to improve and exploit their estates commercially, following the remarkable lead of the 6th Earl of Mar at Alloa, his kinsman Sir John Erskine at Alva, and George Abercromby at Tullibody. Coal mines, bleaching greens, mills, canals, breweries and harbours testify to hard-headed practicality, and provided a profitable corrective to Jacobitism. Indeed, the lack of support for the Stewart cause can be inferred from the fact that *the Earl of Mar, with all his popularity, could not raise three men in his own town of Alloa* to support his 1715 rebellion.

Alloa later became one of Britain's first industrial towns, and carries the traces of a medium-scale Victorian prosperity. It was too far up the Forth to aspire to greater. Philanthropic burgesses generated grandiose but now forgotten civic buildings, and commissioned opulent and lavishly crafted houses for themselves and their establishments.

The Ochils, extending eastwards from Blairlogie to the Firth of Tay, are most dominant above Clackmannanshire's Hillfoot villages, and their omnipresence generates a peculiar loyalty to the settlements on its slopes from their natives. A common characteristic of each of these ancient communities is the old Statute Labour Road passing through the upper part of each village. It was superseded by the new Stirling to Kinross turnpike road in 1806, and stretches of it now offer a pleasurable walk. Its existence, however, is a key to understanding the growth of these towns. Blairlogie is Arcadia; Menstrie more homespun and slightly schizophrenic; Alva and Tillicoultry form the basis of the Hillfoots Mill Heritage Trail; Dollar is an unlikely, classical Enlightenment transplant to Arcadia, now frayed at the edges; whilst Muckhart's seclusion accounts for

Opposite: Devon Colliery Beam Engine (Fowler).

Coal and local wealth were long synonymous. First gathered on the Forth banks by monks, coal was the *raison d'être* for Gartmorn Dam, Sauchie and industrial Alloa. Extracted by Earls of Mar, Robert Bald, Bruce of Kennet and the Alloa Coal Company, who prospered; speculated on by Schaws of Sauchie, Bruces of Clackmannan, Erskines of Alva and Taits of Harviestoun, who failed. John Ramsay of Ochtertyre recorded *It is said that Clackmannanshire colliers, in their Litany, used to pray for heavy rains in July, to spoil the west country people's peats;* for the Stirlingshire tenants otherwise relied on Alloa coal for warmth and for fertiliser via their limekilns. Prior to 1900, there were 70 named, and about 200 unnamed shafts in the County. By 1946 there were 18. With great optimism, huge new coal pits were opened in the 1950s necessitating the import of complete communities from Lanarkshire, creating the metamorphosis of Tullibody, Sauchie, Coalsnaughton and Fishcross. Their subsequent closure left Clackmannanshire without its oldest indigenous industry, and many miners without work.

The River Devon rises behind Alva's Ben Cleuch (the highest Ochil Peak) and, as a gushing stream, winds eastwards through Perthshire's Glendevon until she aptly reaches the Crook of Devon in Kinross-shire. With sudden turn westwards she changes character, rushing along craggy ravines and tossing through the chasms and falls of Rumbling Bridge gorge and Cauldron Linn. Later, more gracious, she meanders through the Hillfoots valley, absorbing each village stream, before encircling Tullibody, and slouching into the Forth at Cambus. For a journey of over 30 miles, she is only 5¼ miles from her source.

the survival of its atmosphere as representing the rural dream. Inexplicably, Rumbling Bridge gorge has forfeited its fame as a beauty spot, although it retains the beauty and is now more accessible than ever before (unlike neighbouring Cauldron Linn). Glendevon has been included for the pure enjoyment of a remote highland glen so close to industrialised Scotland.

Organisation of this Book

This Guide opens with a description of Clackmannan, the historic county town, with its hinterland. Alloa is described from the shore to the modern centre, followed by its outer suburbs and the adjoining villages of Sauchie and Fishcross. Thereafter the Guide, like an African explorer, traces the river Devon from outfall to source: from its meeting with the Forth at Cambus near Tullibody, past Blairlogie, Menstrie, Alva, Tillicoultry and Dollar, to Muckhart and its nearby beauty spots, up to its source in Glendevon. It is possible to explore the best of the district in a weekend, but well worth while returning.

The small numbers adjacent to the text are keyed into the maps. Where possible, each principal entry follows the order of name, location, architect (if known), date and description. The index should facilitate cross-referencing.

Right of Access

The majority of the buildings in this Guide are visible from public roads or footpaths. However, few of them are normally open for public visiting, and readers are requested to respect the occupiers' privacy.

Stobie's map of Clackmannanshire in 1783.

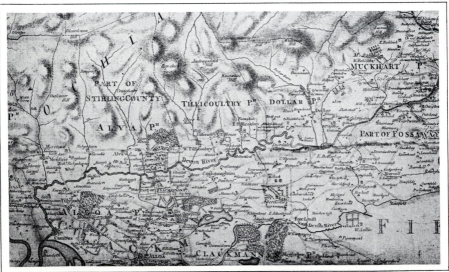

Dollar Academy

Fowler

Clackmannan Tower and Parish Church along the ridge of King's Seat Hill.

Like Stirling and Edinburgh, Clackmannan is built with a castle at the high point (King's Seat Hill to the west) and the town's main street and market place declining along a ridge to the east. It commands a superb view over the upper Forth to Stirling and the Highlands.

The Tower was never a royal fortress. Its early life as a royal hunting seat ended with its sale to Robert Bruce in 1359. The town only became a burgh of barony in the 16th century, by which time its harbour was silting up and the Bruce family had lost its national importance, settling down to its future role as principal landowners in the area.

Judging from the various date stones of houses in the Main Street, the Burgh's greatest period was that of the late 17th century — the period of the construction of the Tolbooth. In 1772 it remained a *small town pleasantly situated on a hill,* with a harbour, where the Black Devon met the Forth (newly improved by Sir Lawrence Dundas to achieve a mean depth of 10 ft). But the port of Alloa had expanded and superseded that of Clackmannan. By 1802 Alexander Campbell could record *the wretched appearance of the houses* which formed *a striking contrast to the beauty and grandeur of the scenery around it. Without trade of artificers, this village is fast hastening to decay.* A fashionable new Parish Church in 1815 might be thought to have heralded a revival of some kind. Unfortunately not. The Burgh's fine Tolbooth became *a heap of ruins and a nuisance to the public,* and the Sheriff Court was transferred to Alloa in 1822. In 1837 Robert Chambers found *an old decayed and deserted town with one long unpaved street;* little improvement was visible 50 years later.

Contemporary Clackmannan differs in that the houses have been repaired and there are new suburbs. It conveys a slightly eerie sensation of being a town of

Aerial view of Clackmannan.

RCAHMS

national potential whose time never came. It is that feeling which makes the trip from the Castle (negotiating barbed wire, cow and dog), down to the church and the main street — always with view over the Forth or north to the Ochils — so very worthwhile.

Clackmannan Tower, from 14th century
King's Seat Hill, a spectacular and strategic site in the control of the Forth, was sold with its hunting lodge by King David II to a kinsman, Robert Bruce, in 1359 (possibly to keep it in the family without it continuing a royal burden). The great rectangular tower, constructed of beautifully cut blocks of pink sandstone, was begun soon afterwards to the normal pattern of ground floor cellars, great hall above, capped by a guard house. In the 15th century, a taller square tower, built equally delectably, was added abutting the south, at which time both were presented with a crenellated wall-walk supported on machicolations (open corbels between which defenders could pour unpleasantness upon attackers).

In the late 16th century, the Bruces built a splendid mansion block with crowstep gables and turrets to the south-west; and in the late 17th century, a new entrance court, walled and protected by a moat, to the east, with a new doorway into the castle embellished by a lovely pedimented frame. Fragments of the outer walls, of a garden terrace, and of an ancient bowling green may still be traced.

The direct Bruce line died with Lady Catherine Bruce in 1791, soon after which the mansion crumbled and the stones thriftily resetted elsewhere. The Tower itself was later threatened by coal mining subsidence. Although that threat has receded, access is not easy, internal access currently impossible and the environs a tragic waste of outstanding potential.

Clackmannan Tower.
Below: The Tower with adjoining mansion, 1807.

Clackmannan Parish Church.

RCAHMS

Clackmannan Parish Church, James Gillespie Graham, 1815
There has been a church or a chapel at Clackmannan since St Serf visited from Culross in the 8th century. The first stone church, consecrated by Bishop David de Bernham of St Andrews in 1249, may have been the one around which the present kirk was constructed in 1815. Gillespie Graham was a fashionable choice of architect and he rose to the occasion and fine site (which he did not always do — see Doune in *Stirling and the Trossachs*). It is a fairly delicate, standard regency box in perpendicular Gothic with a buttressed tower plonked symmetrically against the west gable. A fine plaque by Sir Robert Lorimer commemorates the Master of Burleigh, who fell at Le Château in 1914, the German wooden cross having been brought from his grave. The adjacent **Manse,** 1741, one of the larger houses in the town, contains fine Adam-style fireplaces in the public rooms.

High Street, County Architect, W. H. Henry, 1950s
High Street connects the Tower with the Market Place, lined on the north by a complete row of 18th century cottages built in rows, blocks and around courtyards, wholly reconstructed in the 1950s. The architect re-used many details from the original houses including skewputts, pantiles, corbelled corners of old stonework, datestones and plaques. **No. 2** has a plaque dated 1702, and a two-sided sundial set into a corner stone; **No. 4** a lintel dated 1668 and 1738; **No. 44-46** has scrolled skewputts. **Kirk Wynd, Port Street** and **Garden Place** were rebuilt at the same time, and one corner of Garden Place has an almost identical gable to one in High Street, with uneven skewputts and corbelled stonework. Civic Trust Award 1959.

The Bruce Family
The end of the 17th century saw the beginning of decline of the Bruces of Clackmannan. From the 1650s Sir Henry Bruce developed the extensive coalfields of Clackmannan, being fortunate in having coal seams near the harbour, but the costs of draining the seams below the level of the Forth and Black Devon were great. Sir Henry spent much time and money trying to solve this problem, building a water-powered *Egyptian Wheel,* an early bucket-and-chain pump. He died in 1674 leaving immense debts to his son, David Bruce. The latter, as well as holding the office of Hereditary Sheriff, became Member of Parliament to Charles II and later James VII and II: but by refusing to take the oaths to the government of William and Mary, he was removed in 1693. Meanwhile the collieries were poorly managed and David Bruce was declared bankrupt in 1708. To pay his creditors, he sold the estate and the Sheriffdom to Colonel William Dalrymple, 2nd son of the Earl of Stair. David died in Clackmannan in 1712, and his son Henry, 15th Baron of Clackmannan, came out for Prince Charles Edward in the 1745 uprising. He died in 1772, but his widow Catherine Bruce of Newton continued to live in the old mansion and Tower until her death.

CLACKMANNAN

Below: Lady Catherine Bruce.
Right: The Market Cross and Stone of Mannan in 1861, the original High Street houses are behind.
Below right: 3 Port Street, now demolished, had a wall doocot and a crowstep sundial.

Lady Catherine Bruce entertained Robert Burns in September 1787 dressed, it is said, with a tartan scarf and the white rose of the Stuarts. This lady was renowned for conferring the honour of knighthood upon distinguished guests with the great two-handed sword of her ancestor King Robert Bruce. After knighting Burns, her toast was *Hooi uncos*, or *away strangers*.

He who wishes to see things that will shortly be found no more, should visit Clackmannan Castle. There he will still find the house, the furniture, and the environs in all the simplicity of former times, yet not without an air of dignity; and what is more rare and precious, he will see in the lady a living specimen of the style and manners of the last age. John Ramsay of Ochtertyre.

Fowler

The Market Place

Where the High Street descending from the Castle crosses the ancient road from Kincardine to Alloa it broadens as the Market Place, marked by the Market Cross, the Stone of Mannan, and the tower of the ruined Tolbooth. Thence, shaped like a wedge of cheese, it becomes **Main Street,** narrowing until plugged, like a cork in a bottle, by the 1903 Town Hall at the bottom.

The Market Place leading into Main Street.

The Market Cross, 16th century

A single trefoil shaft, bearing the arms of Bruce at the top. Until the Tolbooth was built the prisoners awaiting trial were chained to the Cross, the frotting of the chains being the reason for the slenderness of the shaft towards the base.

The Tolbooth, from 1592

All that now remains of the Tolbooth is the late 17th century Belfry tower. William Menteith, Sheriff of Clackmannan had presented a petition to parliament requesting that a Tolbooth be built, since he and his predecessors had *been compelled to hold courts openly at the Market Cross of Clackmannan . . . and keep inward the transgressors and malefactors within his dwelling house.* An Act was duly passed authorising its construction and the gathering of taxes *to the sum of twa hundred fourscore and four punds.* The bell, presented by Sir Lawrence Dundas in 1765, was rung each evening at 6 pm until 1939. By 1792, the Tolbooth and courthouse had become that *heap of ruins and a nuisance to the public,* and was wholly abandoned by 1822.

On 6th July 1699, Robert Livingstone, chapman at Crook of Devon, pleaded guilty to stealing a black tup and two wedder sheep, and was sentenced *to be stripped naked of his clothes, and scourged by the hand of the hangman through the whole town of Clackmannan with one of the sheep's heads and four feet hanging about his neck, and thereafter to be banished out the said shire.*

CLACKMANNAN

The Royal Oak Hotel.

The **Main Street** contains some fine 18th and 19th century houses, with the occasional one — such as a Post Office with its interesting wrought iron gutter brackets — converted to a shop. The curved gable of the **Royal Oak Hotel,** c. 1700, recalls Clackmannanshire's extensive trade with the Low Countries, the name itself that of a locally owned 18th century ship, a painting of which once hung in the Tower. Gap sites on both sides of Main Street, about halfway along, have been infilled with suitable houses by the County Architect, W. H. Henry, 1970. The new cottages on the south side have a pend leading through to similar housing at Garden Place.

Town Hall, 1903, Ebenezer Simpson
This Art Nouveau red sandstone two-storey block closing Main Street was gifted by John Thomson Paton to provide a library, billiards and reading rooms in front of the 1888 Town Hall by Adam Frame. Double and triple Gothic windows have transoms, a pedimented crest frowns over the entrance and there is Art Nouveau lettering and sculptured architraves. The four rainwater heads between the windows are decorated with different animals.

Little historic remains in **North Street,** although the scale is light and airy, and there is the odd stone warehouse. The front part of the Drill Hall was once the *Penny School* of Clackmannan, each pupil contributing one penny towards his education.

The Name Clackmannan is derived from *Clack* signifying stone, church or village, and *Mannan* being an ancient district of Scotland around the head of the River Forth where the sea-god *Manau* was worshipped. The *Stone of Mannan* was worshipped by ancient pagans who believed it contained the spirit of the sea-god. The original position of the stone was at Lookaboutye Brae, probably once the shore of the Forth. Later it was brought to the centre of the Burgh and in 1833 it was raised onto a whinstone plinth which was dragged from the Abbey Craig at Stirling by Bruce of Kennet and sixteen stout horses.

The credulous enjoy a story told to explain the origins of the name *Clackmannan* and of the County motto *Look about ye.* King Robert Bruce had been hunting in the Forest of Clackmannan, and on returning to the Tower discovered that he had lost his glove. With the instruction *Look about ye,* he sent his followers to search for the glove *(or mannan),* which was found by the stone *(or clack)* on the brae *(Lookaboutye Brae)* to the south of the town.

Kirk Wynd forms the northern wing of the historic Alloa to Kincardine road, named after being graced with two Secession churches: the Relief Church, founded in 1788 following dissatisfaction by the Parish with their Minister, and the Free Church built after the Disruption in 1843. Both were abandoned at the Triple Union in 1932: the Relief demolished in 1933, and the Free, designed by John Burnet in 1845, now the Masonic Lodge. **Mayfield House,** 1862, by John Melvin, at the corner of North Street, is a simple classical bay-fronted house built as the Manse of the Free (Mayfield) Church. **Erskine House,** c. 1830, the former Relief Manse, is a delightful two-storey classical house with pilastered door, and architraves above ground floor windows, set in a large walled garden.

Clackmannan House, c. 1815, is a classical two-storey house with basement and attic. There is an exceptional doorway, with Tuscan columns and pilasters and fanlight, in a ground floor of rusticated grey free-stone.

Inch of Ferryton marks the site of what was once probably an island on the Forth, at the crossing point by ferry to Dunmore on the opposite bank. The Stone of Mannan may once have rested here before being moved first to **Lookaboutye Brae,** on the old road out of Clackmannan, and from there to its present site.

Clackmannan Colliery, c. 1800, showing the water wheel, wagon road and coal workings, drawn by John Clerk of Eldin for Sir George Clerk of Penicuik.

National Museums of Scotland

Kennet House, Thomas Harrison, c. 1795 (demolished)

Built *in a style of elegance and simplicity that marks the taste and judgement of the owner* (Alexander Bruce of Kennet), this classical mansion, with side wings, its bowed Tuscan porch answering its segment headed Tuscan columned tripartite windows, was *situated amid pleasure gardens and plantations of great beauty, on a rising ground overlooking the basin of the Forth.* An unusual oval lodge marks the entrance to a long, curving avenue.

Clackmannan Colliery

From the 1650s the carselands between Clackmannan and the Forth were explored for coal by Sir Henry Bruce. William Dalrymple, who came into possession in 1708, provided the colliery with a water-powered drainage wheel and lined the Pow (port) at the mouth of the Black Devon with stone blocks to improve the landing place for loading coal into flat-bottomed boats. After 1742, Sir Laurence Dundas, the next owner (whose family became Marquises of Zetland), built a sea wall from the Pow down to Kennetpans where there was a more substantial harbour. In 1770 he constructed a wagon road from his mines to Kennetpans, rebuilt the harbour, and straightened the course of Black Devon itself two years later. Little now remains. **Craigrie Farm** is on the location of the main pit, the Speedwell pit being further west. The old lade which served the water wheels at these pits can still be made out in places.

RCAHMS

Kennet House.

I was one week at Kennet where I spent my time very pleasantly — no appearance of famine or straits there. A very pleasant house were they a little further from the coals; but they are mending in that respect. John Ramsay of Ochtertyre. *Letters*

Right: Kennet Village.

Kennet Village
A complete row of twenty late 18th century miners' cottages, built by the Bruce family for miners at Kennet Colliery. Well built of cut stone, with pantiled roofs, the cottages were restored by the District Council as a fine example of an 18th century miners' row.

Kennetpans was formerly a salt panning community on the banks of the Forth. In mediaeval times salt was mainly used for preserving food for winter consumption, and the first panning was undertaken by small communities of monks, evaporating the water from the salt in large cast iron pans over coal-fired furnaces. The practice continued until the late 18th century.

Distillery ruins at Kennetpans.

Kennetpans House 1783

Only the walled kitchen garden survives of John Stein's mansion: the lawns are now marshy wasteland.

Broadcarse Farmhouse, nearby, is a late 18th century two-storey farm with symmetrically planned side wings.

RCAHMS

The Garlet, near Kilbagie, c. 1700 (demolished)

Most likely built after Alexander Bruce, a second son of the Kennet family, received the estate from his father, the Garlet was an attractive small mansion with crowsteps, pantiles and quoins, distinguished by a projecting entrance gable at the centre of the facade with a pilastered entrance, heraldic panel and round attic window.

Kilbagie

Site of the Steins' principal distillery before 1776, which, at its peak, produced more than 3,000 tons of spirit annually from over 60,000 bolls of grain. The *draff* or waste grain fed 7,000 cattle and 2,000 pigs. The distillery buildings covered over three acres of ground and employed more than three hundred men. By 1795 the distillery had been sold by James Stein's creditors for under one fifth of its cost, but that family were in business again at Kilbagie in the early 1800s. The spirit was shipped from the harbour at Kennetpans (then a free port) and transported to the harbour along a canal, now known as the Canal Burn. The Distillery survived until the middle of the 19th century, then becoming a chemical plant for a short period, before being put to its present use as a paper mill.

By the 1770s James and John Stein, farmers on the Kennet Estate, had established distilleries at Kennetpans and at nearby Kilbagie, using local supplies of grain and fuel to produce gin for the London market, shipped from Kennetpans harbour. The Steins' distilleries proved so successful that their London rivals sought to put them out of business. In the 1780s, a number of laws were passed to increase the taxation on spirits produced in Scotland. By 1790 the yearly taxation per gallon of every still used for distillation was 2/6d in England, while in Scotland it had risen to a staggering £9 sterling. Before these new taxes were enforced, the two distilleries together contributed more money in taxation to the Government than the whole of the Scottish land tax. All that remains today is a fascinating group of ruins.

The Garlet.

Kilbagie House.

CDC Tech Services

KILBAGIE

In *The Jolly Beggars,* Burns apostrophised Kilbagie Whisky:

Despise that shrimp, that withered imp,
With a' his noise an' cap 'rin;
An' take a share with those that bear
The budget and the apron!
And by that stowp! my faith an' houpe,
And by that **dear Kilbagie,**
If e'er ye want, or meet wi' scant,
May I ne'er weet my craigie.

Kilbagie was *a peculiar sort of whisky . . ., a great favourite with Poosie Nansie's clubs.*

Mill House, Kilbagie.

Andrew Meikle, an Alloa engineer invented a threshing machine which was first constructed by his son George, at Kilbagie in 1787. It consisted of a simple device of rollers, one equipped with blades, which removed the grain from the straw mechanically, the grain falling through a mesh, and the straw being pulled out of the machine by another roller.

Right: Cast iron sluice gate at Forestmill.
Below: Cottage, Linn Mill.

Kilbagie Mills, 1874
Converted to a paper mill by J. A. Weir Ltd., and still operated by Weirs for Gestetner, the buildings include some surviving rubble-built distillery buildings. The complex is dominated by a huge brick water tower. Within the complex are the remains of a circular doocot, one of a pair, with the date and initials W B D 1859.

Kilbagie House, c. 1776, the fairly plain dwelling of James Stein, is decorated with a single attic porthole, moulded doorways and club skewputts. The west addition, c. 1800, is bow fronted with a shaped gable. Nearby are rusticated gate piers.

Linn Mill

The site (since 1690) of two ancient grain mills on the Black Devon, near Grassmainston Farm, now survived only by a group of small 18th century cottages, the west-most one being the archetype of the traditional cottage — two small windows, centre door, crow-stepped gable, and pantiled roof with slate skirting.

Forestmill

Originally a hamlet, or fermtoun, of a grain mill, on the Black Devon within the Clackmannan Forest. In 1766 the teacher at the local school was Michael Bruce, author of the poem *Lochleven.* Note the splendid corrugated iron village hall.

The water for Gartmorn Dam is drawn off the Black Devon along a lade just to the south of the village. The large weir and sluice gates are of early 18th century origin.

Fowler

Brucefield House c. 1724 (with slightly later wing) Built by Alexander Bruce of Kennet, Brucefield is the only surviving 18th century mansion in the district. The slate roofs are hipped and steeply pitched, with tall prominent chimney stacks in the manner of the grand early country houses of Scotland, introduced after the Restoration by Sir William Bruce of Kinross. The entrance, now through a Doric-columned porchway on the west front, was formerly at first floor level on the east front, commemorated by a window. It was beautifully restored, after a long period of neglect, by James Shearer of Dunfermline, a fine architect in the Arts and Crafts mould. **The Stable Block** of Brucefield Mains, late 18th century, is a very pleasing open square, white harled with pantiled roofs.

Hartshaw Farm near Brucefield, 18th century, is a U-shaped whitewashed cottage, with pantiles and gabled attic dormers. Nearby pantiled **Hartshaw Mill,** built as a corn mill in the early 1700s, is now used for storage. The mill cannibalised stone from **Hartshaw Tower,** a 15th century seat of the Stewarts of Rosyth, and the cottage's west wing has an inscribed stone initialled R.O.S., dated 1574.

Brucefield House.
Below: The Stable Block, Brucefield Mains.

Brucefield

About 1724 Alexander Bruce of Kennet . . . set about making a new place at Brucefield. It was seemingly a wild undertaking to set down a house upon the top of a moor without a tree. The want of natural beauties was the most striking for its being so near a rich variegated country. In the garden . . . the last Kennet used to raise the earliest and best kitchen crops in the country. It may, however, be questioned whether the family gained essentially by making Brucefield. The same money and attention bestowed upon their old seat three score years ago, would have made a far better return. . . . About 1758 or 1759 Lord Kennet sold Brucefield to the late James Abercromby. Ramsay MSS.

Brucefield, the residence of Sir Ralph Abercromby's father, has nothing either of convenience or ornament to recommend it to notice.
Alexander Campbell, 1802.

CDC Tech Services

RIAS Library

Alloa in 1672, drawn by Captain John Slezer.

The Erskines of Mar

From the time of their arrival in Alloa in the 14th century, the Erskines played a major role in the history of Scotland. For loyalty to David II, Sir Robert Erskine was appointed Keeper of the royal castles of Stirling, Edinburgh and Dumbarton; the present Earl of Mar is still hereditary keeper of Stirling Castle. The 3rd Lord Erskine was made responsible for the safety of the young James V (Stirling Castle being chosen as the safest retreat) after the fall of James IV at Flodden (1513). For six years the young Mary Queen of Scots resided with the Erskine family, before being taken to France. It was at Alloa House that Queen Mary reconciled with Darnley when she granted the 5th Lord the long-sought title of Earl of Mar, one month before her wedding in 1565.

One tradition holds that whilst Mary was visiting Alloa her infant son died, and it was a substituted infant of the Earl of Mar who was to become James VI and I: a tradition reinforced by the strong facial likeness of the Stewarts to the Erskines.

1 **Alloa Tower,** from 15th century
Neglected, inaccessible, barely visible, sadly overshadowed by a factory complex, its once celebrated pleasure grounds now a housing estate, the Tower is one of the largest in Scotland and formed the home of one of the country's most distinguished families — the Erskines, Earls of Mar.

The Tower is all that remains of a grand complex. The great house, adjoining the Tower, *sumptuously furnished* according to Sir Robert Sibbald in 1692, was burnt out in August 1800 with grievous loss of historic portraits and furnishings. Its successor, a classical mansion, 1834-38 by George Angus, and much Victorianised by John Melvin, was demolished in 1959.

The Erskines were granted Alloa as their principal seat in 1363, and the great Tower and associated defences must already have been complete by the time of the first reference to a *Manor or Castle* at Alloa in a 1497 charter. Its current curious appearance is the result of rows of 18th century windows punched through the eleven feet thick wall, and the wall walk and roundels at the top. Its ancient roof survives inside. Prior to the improvements, the Tower consisted of a first floor Great Hall, private apartments above, and a guardroom in the roof space, all connected by a turnpike stair in the thickness of the south-west corner, still lit by the original slit windows. The huge hall was later split into two levels, a new semi-circular, domed staircase added, and the new main door enriched by Ionic pilasters, a pediment and the sculpted Erskine crest and motto *Je pense plus* — all almost certainly designed by the 6th Earl.

The Erskines of Mar were great improvers, and had not the estates been forfeited after the 1715 rebellion, the history of Alloa could have been significantly different. Improvements to the Tower were in hand by 1672 when it was sketched by Captain John Slezer. The drawing shows the keep with a great courtyard of tall buildings to the east, and older ones to the south, clearly meriting the praise lavished upon it by travellers during the 18th century. Defoe, for example, in 1723 thought *the Castle of Alloa is now so beautified, the buildings, and especially the gardens so completely modern that no appearance of a castle can be said to remain . . . The gardens are by much the finest in Scotland and not outdone by many in England. There is, in a word, everything that nature and art can do brought to perfection.*

It is difficult, now, to form a picture of this pleasure ground. Mar obtained the advice of Louis XIV's gardener Le Nôtre, and the layout was of a formality of planned vistas which earned it Pennant's description of *extensive gardens planted in the old style.* It dated mostly from 1706 (although William Boutcher was working there to Mar's design in 1722), and consisted of *long avenues, clipped hedges, statues and ornaments.*

Of all this nothing remains save the potential to recreate — despite the new houses on part of the land. The keep is boarded up, largely inaccessible and mostly derelict, and the surrounding landscape

Alloa Tower in 1788 by David Allan. Part of the mansion can be made out behind.

The last Earl of Mar had a great turn for architecture and was always ready to give his neighbours advice. Tullibody, Tillicoultry and Blairdrummond Houses are said to have been built upon his plans. The Rebellion of 1715 broke out ere his additions to Alloa House were finished. Ramsay MSS.

Alloa Tower.

Bobbing John, the 6th Earl, became the father of industrial Alloa by his development of the harbour, Customs House, coal mines and the construction of Gartmorn Dam to provide water power to drain the mines. The Dam's water powered the driveshaft of Alloa's industry (but is now contaminated by open-cast mines). Secretary of State for Scotland to Queen Anne, Mar was dismissed under suspicion for Jacobitism by the Hanoverians. He returned to Scotland and became Commander-in-Chief to James VIII, ineptly leading the Jacobite forces at the ill-fated Battle of Sheriffmuir in 1715. He went into exile and died impoverished in France in 1732. His forfeited estates were bought by his brother Lord Grange who restored them to the family.

From his exile, the Earl restlessly planned and re-designed his estates, Stirling Castle, houses in France and, so his sketch books reveal, plans for a new town at Edinburgh and a Forth and Clyde Canal.

However blamable the last Earl of Mar might be as a statesman and general he falls to be considered as a pattern for a great man who wishes to establish a family interest founded on the good will and affection of his neighbours. He was always ready to serve (his neighbours) in small as well as in great matters without seeming to expect anything in return and his manners were uniformly gracious and easy at home and abroad.
Ramsay MSS.

Top: The Earl of Mar's additions to Alloa Tower, designed in 1727: the finest Baroque Palace in Scotland. South-west and north-east elevations.
Middle: 1780s engraving of the mansion from the south. What had been built of the Baroque ornamentation did not survive for long.
Bottom: The 7th Earl of Mar and family, 1783, by David Allan. The eldest son was painted out and replaced by the top hat in the tree after a family disagreement.

Scottish Record Office

conveys the feeling of Pompeii before excavation: dormant but inherently magical.

2 The 1852 **Stable Block** is characterised by a tower above the northern arched entrance, and the walls of
3 the garden survive yet.

CDC Libraries

National Galleries of Scotland

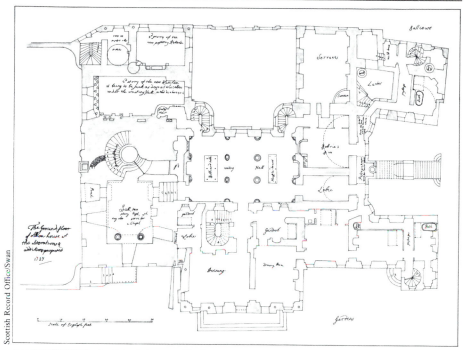

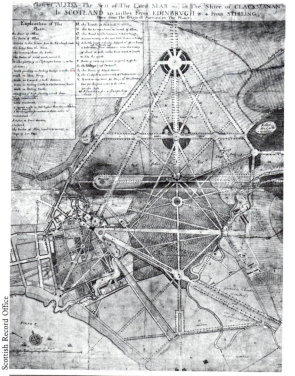

He proceeded upon a great scale. His gardens at Alloa were in the Dutch taste, on the model of Hampton Court, the favourite residence of King William. They were nicely kept, a master gardener and twelve men being constantly employed till after the forfeiture. But though much visited and admired they were too magnificent and expensive to be imitated by the country gentlemen of those times. By their means, perhaps the rearing and trimming of hedges was first introduced among us.
Ramsay MSS.

Above: Ground floor plans of the Earl's additions, 1727. The keep became a chapel, other features included a *Waiting Hall* with shuffleboard and billiard table, *pully chairs* or lifts, bathrooms, the two-storey *Great Sallon,* and a reservoir on the roof which also powered the fountains in the gardens.

Left: Estate plan by Bernard Lens, 1710. Each vista or walk centred on a distant landmark. The town and house are to the left; the parks, meadows and woods stretch towards Sauchie and Clackmannan.

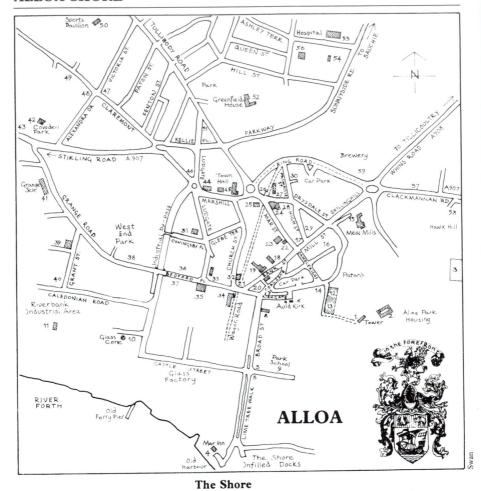

ALLOA

The Shore

It is almost impossible, now, to appreciate the importance of Alloa's harbour and ferry to its growth as an 18th century industrial town. First mentioned in 1502, the harbour expanded in importance with the arrival of the Customs House, responsible for all upper Forth ports, in 1710. Defoe found a good harbour thirteen years later wherein the Glasgow merchants were proposing to erect export warehouses. In 1772, Pennant found the harbour exporting over one third of Scotland's total coal production, and by 1800 it was handling 7,241 tons of shipping each year, employing 500 seamen. The harbour was attractive to traders for its rough hewn stone quay, double tide and safe anchorage. Four years later, during the Napoleonic Wars, it was noted, approvingly, as being able to take warships of up to 40 guns.

The successful harbour brought industry (in 1843 there were proposals to bridge the Forth at this point),

The River Forth at Alloa, mid 19th century.

CDC Libraries

and soon it was handling 2,000 vessels per annum. However, silting and its relative isolation made it vulnerable to faster methods of transport; made redundant by railways and roads, it was infilled in 1951, before the growth of leisure and tourism indicated a better alternative future.

4 **Mar Inn,** pre-1744
Marooned like the Admiral Benbow, and wired off from the Forth, the Inn was probably built for travellers on the Craigward (or King's) Ferry, a very busy river crossing slightly upstream. The Inn was refaced in the 19th century into the plain, harled, two-storey block it is now.

Fowler

Lime Tree Walk
Lime Tree Walk was formed by the Earl of Mar as a formal route from Alloa to the harbour, very similar to a comparable walk between Dundee and its harbour (see *Dundee* volume in this series). The upper end, originally called John's Street and latterly Broad Street, was planned by Mar as the eastern flank of a new town. Of this fine promenade, nothing original survives. The **Manse,** now reinstated into a discotheque, had a 1714 date stone. Defoe found Lime Tree Walk *very spacious, well built, with rows of trees planted all the way* so much so that he took it for the High Street of Alloa — as maybe Mar intended it to be. The Limes and spaciousness survive yet, in altered but recoverable circumstances. The only built

CDC Libraries

5 survivals are the extraordinary **Gate Piers,** erected in 1714. The outer piers have a quatrefoil plan and are topped with tall pyramidal finials set on balls. The inner piers were probably built in 1838.

Top: The Mar Inn.
Above: The Ferry Pier before it was abandoned in the 1930s. The Glassworks are behind.
Below: Lime Tree Walk.

David Allan (1744-96), son of the Alloa harbour master, was brought up at the Shore. The young Allan's artistic talents came to the notice of Lady Cathcart of Schawpark and she, with her friends Mrs Abercromby of Tullibody and Lady Frances Erskine, sponsored him at Art schools in Glasgow and Rome. In Rome, Allan was the first Scotsman to be awarded the Gold Medal for historical composition. Allan gifted works to his benefactors, as illustrated in the following letter to Lady Frances Erskine, accompanying classical works for both herself and Mr Abercromby in 1773.

Former favours I have already received naturally invites me to send something to Alloa in my way of painting, and write that I am well, and never forget the generous assistance which my benefactor has been pleased to grant in placing me in this first and noblest school in Rome, which may lead me to improvement in that fine art of painting. . . . I hope by degrees to let all my friends have some of my pictures.

Fowler

The Wagon Road, 1768
Coal from Sauchie was pulled in wagons or carts with cast iron wheels, three at a time by ponies, along a wagon road which ended at Alloa Harbour (although later extended to the Glassworks). Parts survive as a footpath between Primrose Street and the former Burgh School, with brick arches under the streets.

CDC Libraries

The old Market Place, now under Paton's Mills. The *land* on the left, c. 1700, was the *Speaker's Lodgings.*

Thomas Tucker, reporting to Oliver Cromwell of a visit to Alloa in 1655: *On the north side of the Firth, there is a pretty fine burgh called Alloway, having a fine harbour, and an excellent coale, which is for the most part shipped out and carried away by the Dutch, there being noe vessell belonging to the place. Nevertheless, there hath usually beene a pretty trade for that commodity. The towne of Kennet, likewise, is a very good greate coale, but chiefly sent from port to port, and never seldome outwards.*

The Old Town of Alloa
The town is pleasant, well built and full of trade recorded Daniel Defoe in 1723. Full of trade indeed, for it had little other claim to fame; the heart of the old parish being Tullibody to the west, and the town only a burgh of barony. It was thus the creature of these energetic feu superiors, the Earls of Mar, who had a vested interest in promulgating trade. That being Alloa's *raison d'être,* its subsequent history should raise no eyebrows: for, with the exception of two buildings, the entire old town of Alloa, with its market place, lies beneath, and within the fief of Paton's Mills and Candleriggs car park, and Maclay's Brewery.

By the close of the 17th century it consisted of a few narrow streets and Market Place, by the bridge over the Brothie Burn: but the burn was also the means of powering industry, and in a conflict between the old town of Alloa, and industry, industry always won. During the 18th century, some of the southern properties were demolished for extensions to Alloa House pleasure grounds, and to compensate, the Erskines feued to the west (Forth Street), and to the north (Mar Street). The main road to Clackmannan was re-aligned to the north, and now comprises the town's commercial spine of Shillinghill, Mill Street, and Bank Street.

By 1800 the town was busily engaged in making *glass bottles, bricks, tiles, tanning, tobacco manufacture, camblets, broad cloth, linen, muslin, iron works and coal export,* particular attention being drawn to *the ingenious family of Meikles, engineers and millwrights, well known for their inventions,* who had long settled there. Indeed, the town was possibly more prosperous in 1750 than 50 years later, only picking up population again c. 1840. By then, the new streets were welcomed for their *neat appearance,* but the old ones dismissed as *narrow and irregular.* There was thus no objection when the old Market Place was obliterated in 1867 by Paton's Kilncraigs Mill (on the one side) and Younger's Brewery (on the other); the *Auld Brig* over the Brothie Burn — a haunt of poor repute — soon followed and the Burn now flows beneath Paton's Mill.

Modern Alloa, therefore, is a post-Enlightenment, industrial creation, some old street names surviving around Candleriggs Car Park — Old High Street, Old Bridge Street, Kirkgate, Greenside Street and New Entry. Yet Younger's of Alloa, with their India Export, have vanished like the Market Place; and demolition faces Paton's.

6 **Old Kirk,** Tobias Bauchop, Pat Main, 1680
Only the ruined west gable and bell tower of the old Parish Church of St Mungo remain. The walls of the church have been ashlar, the gable and the lower tower rubble and the top stages ashlar, beneath a delightful bell-shaped roof. The original kirk was in existence by 1401, as a chapel of the church of Clackmannan, not being united with Tullibody as a separate parish until 1600. It was almost totally rebuilt in 1680, with the additional Mar Aisle to the north. The tower shows great similarities to the ruined Tolbooth tower in Clackmannan. A niche in the surviving gable houses a statue of St Mungo. The church was condemned as unsafe in 1816, and stones were used from it in the construction of the new church in Bedford Place. Extensive re-roofing works to the belfry were carried out by the District Council in 1982.

The spacious Kirkyard, dominated by Paton's Mill, contains some fine 18th century memorials within its high rubble walls.

Top: The *Auld Brig* over the Brothy Burn.
Above: The Old Kirk.

Mar and Kellie Mausoleum, Kirkgate, James Gillespie Graham, 1819
Built by the architect of the new Parish Church in the same year, on the site of the old Mar Aisle, the mausoleum is a delicate Gothic rectangle containing memorials to the Mar family from the 16th century. The splendid flower-painted vaulted plaster ceiling is fast deteriorating.

Swan

Tobias Bauchop (or Baak), died 1710, was the most accomplished member of a family of outstanding stone masons working in the area at the close of the 17th century. Tobias reconstructed Alloa Kirk in 1680, and Logie Kirk in 1684, becoming Master Mason to Scotland's first *architect* Sir William Bruce. He was employed at Bruce's own Kinross House (from 1687), and later at Hopetoun House, Craigiehall and Mertoun. Bauchop is best remembered for his Dumfries Town House built in 1705.

Top: Bauchop's House.
Right: Stripehead and Kirkgate before redevelopment.
Below: Sundial, Bauchop's House.

RIAS Library

7 **Bauchop's House,** 25 Kirkgate, Tobias Bauchop, 1695
The finest town house in Clackmannanshire, built in finely pointed ashlar. The carved stonework is of magnificent quality. All openings have delicate moulded architraves with lugs. Above the doorway is a garlanded shield with the initials TB and ML and 1695 — Tobias Bauchop and Margaret Lapsley (or Lindsay) and a finely carved sundial supported by (according to Crawford) *the only authentic, petrified portrait of Auld Nick in existance.* Recently restored to its former glory with the help of the National Trust for Scotland and the District Council.

Opposite, encompassing Kirkgate once again with a well scaled sense of enclosure, are new flats by the District Architects, in a graceful rhythm of pink tinted blockwork.

CDC Libraries

8 **St John's Episcopal Church, Broad Street,** was designed by Sir Rowand Anderson, then plain Robert Anderson, in 1866. Built on the edge of Alloa Park, it is styled in G. G. Scott inspired early geometrical Gothic, and dominated by the impressive broach spire. The rich interior includes a mosaic altarpiece by Salviati. In 1873 Thomas Bradshaw reckoned it to be *the most elegant place of worship in the County,* which still holds true today.

9 **Park School,** William Kerr, 1935
Hall, classrooms and offices accommodated in long, one-storey blocks, in roughcast brick, red tile roof and multi-paned large windows.

CDC Libraries

10 **Alloa Glass Cone,** Glasshouse Loan, 1825
One of three cones built here and the only surviving glass cone in Scotland: a simple round cone of brick, about 60 feet high, on a rubble octagonal base with arched openings.

The large **Maltings** nearby, 1897, are the only buildings that remain of the famous Younger's of Alloa. The bus depot opposite was the Craigward Cooperage of which several buildings remain. The recent cleaning of the sturdy Victorian rubble tenements of **Forbes Street** and **Medwyn Place** reveals their quality.

11 **McKenzie's Carpet Warehouse,**
Kellybank, is an imposing brick palace built in 1920 as offices for the Forth Shipbuilding and Engineering Company, who had prospered during the First World War. In 1919 the two Alloa Shipyards (the Forth and Jeffrey's yards) were bought by Vickers, but were closed for good in 1923 following the post-war depression. During the last twelve years of shipbuilding at Alloa, some 30 steamships of up to 3,500 tons were built.

CDC Tech Services

Top: Broad Street before redevelopment.
Centre: Gatepiers, Lime Tree Walk. The infamous *Bowhouse* housing has gone.
Below: Alloa Glass Cone.

Alloa Glassworks
The United Glass factory is the oldest glassworks in Europe on its original site, founded by Lady Frances Erskine of Mar in 1750 (through the idea of her father, the exiled 6th Earl, who had been impressed with glass-making techniques he had seen in Bohemia). Craftsmen were sought from Bohemia, and the works were established using local raw materials — sand, lime and soda ash. Now the largest glass container factory in the United Kingdom, producing about one and a quarter million bottles every day.

Fowler

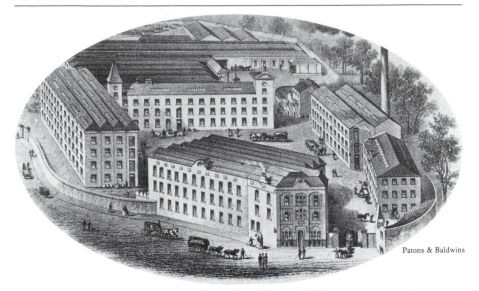

Patons & Baldwins

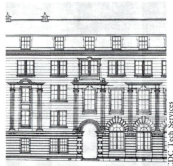

Top: Kilncraigs Mills in 1871.
Above: Part of the west elevation of the 1904 office block.
Below: The 1936 extension.

CDC Tech Services

Kilncraigs Mills, mid 19th century onwards
The precise date of the foundation of this mill is not known, although John Paton was certainly spinning worsted yarns at Kilncraigs by 1814 when he brought the first spinning-Jenny to the mill.

The oldest surviving part is a five-storey classically fronted mill c. 1860. The Burnside Mill (1880s) is a five-storey block, with an impressive eight-storey water tower and a rare wooden cooling tower. The 12 company's pride is evident from the 1904 office block by William Kerr which overlooks the Kirkyard in flamboyant Edwardian baroque, ornamented with tall arched windows, Ionic pilasters and scrolled pediments. Internal enrichments include fine panel work and a wide marble staircase. The adjacent 13 extension by William Kerr, 1936, is possibly the best building of its date and type in Scotland; a white, horizontal, well proportioned block enclosed within two vertically proportioned sections indicating the staircase and amenity rooms.

14 **Paton's Works Canteen** is an agglomeration of Gothic buildings facing Greenside Street all designed by John Melvin. The four-storey square tower was originally built as the **Paton School** in 1864 for the children of millworkers at the bequest of Alexander Paton of Kilncraigs. In 1900, curved gable bays were added to either side, initialled J P S & C (John Paton, Son & Co.). The **Greenside Mission Chapel,** 1873, a simple large chamber with a three-storey Gothic tower, was funded by David Paton of Tillicoultry as a meeting place for the various missionary societies with which he was involved.

Swan

15 **Alloa Meal Mills,** Mill Road, early 19th century
There have been meal mills on this site since at least
the 15th century when *The Mill of Alway* was granted
to the Erskines. There are traces of old stone walls
around the present modern buildings, but the main
elements worth seeing are a date stone *this mill was
built in 1735* rebuilt into the north gable, and a rare
view of the Brothie Burn, before it disappears into the
Paton and Baldwin complex. Some Alloa feus still
oblige corn to be ground at this Mill: difficult to
comply with since it functions solely as a grain store.
A 1668 marriage lintel and a 1770 Blacksmith's panel
are built into walls at the junction of Old High Street
and Old Bridge Street.

Maclay's Thistle Brewery, 1870
One of the last independent Victorian breweries still
functioning in Scotland, operating from a friendly, but
not outstanding, range of brick buildings dominated
by the weathervaned square tower of the brewhouse.
16 The **Office Block,** facing East Vennel, 1896, is
distinguished by round windows and mouldings.

John Melvin & Son
The Melvins were an old Alloa
family, traditionally joiners,
although other branches of the
family established a foundry and a
bicycle works. John Melvin senior
(1805-1884) was the first settled
architect in Alloa, returning to his
native town in 1826 after training
in Edinburgh. He was responsible
for the design (and construction,
continuing the family trade of
joiner) of many houses, villas and
churches in Alloa and district until
his retiral in 1878. John Melvin
junior (1855-1905), having trained
in Edinburgh, joined and continued
his father's business, designing the
majority of Alloa's Victorian villas
— particularly in the west area of
the town.

Maclay's Thistle Brewery.

Fowler

THE TOWN CENTRE

Shillinghill forms the first section of Alloa's
commercial spine, continuing into Mill Street and
Bank Street to the West End. It became the principal
road to Clackmannan after the original route over the
Auld Brig was closed by industrialisation.

It is a long curving street of varying character,
improved now that through traffic has moved to the
by-pass, but requiring both respect and investment.
The District Council's attempt to bring flats back into
the town centre above shops is greatly to be
commended, but more has to be done to woo shoppers
back from Stirling.

Alloa Ale
Beer, which has long been brewed
in Alloa, was developed
commercially to profit from the
population boom of the early 19th
century. By 1900 Alloa contained
Bass Crest, Caponcroft, Forth,
Forthbank, Hutton Park, Meadow,
Mills, Shore, Thistle and
Townhead Breweries; and the
nationally important Younger's
Candleriggs and Arrol's Alloa
Breweries. As a brewing centre, the
town was second only to
Edinburgh, and Edinburgh was
where William McEwan
(1827-1913), son of an Alloa
shipowner, founded his famous
brewery after training in Alloa.
Despite the post-war loss of
overseas markets, and the general
contraction of the brewing
industry, Alloa is fortunate to
retain two famous breweries —
Allied-Lyons' immense Alloa
Brewery and Maclay's small,
independent Thistle Brewery.

CDC Libraries

CDC Libraries

CDC Tech Services

Mill Street contains a selection of two-storey plain 19th century shops and houses, interspaced with more grandiose classical buildings. The **National and Provincial Building Society** (No. 69) retains remnants of the Art Nouveau facade of Fusco's Soda Fountain Cafe, by George Kerr, 1921 which occupies half of a four-storey Renaissance palazzo with beautifully detailed window surrounds, topped by a gabled classical pediment.

W. E. Trent's 1939 Gaumont cinema has an unusually flat plain geometric facade picked out in blue and cream tile work (now a **Bingo Hall**). Trent was house-architect to the Gaumont cinemas in London, and the cinema was partly built on the site of the Savoy Café, where Charles Forte's father taught him the skills that led eventually to T.H.F. On the **Hosiery** by George Kerr, 1903, note the weather cock on its Gothic triangular gable, and the windows rising above a trio of Renaissance round headed windows. (The shop front is a modern disaster.)

41-45 Mill Street, 1874, Adam Frame

Three-storey neo-Grecian of *Greek* Thomson type: the first floor windows with finely moulded windowheads, each topped by an acanthus leaf; and the space between each second floor window decorated with dwarf pilasters over a Greek key pattern. The steep-spired turrets of **26 Mill Street,** a late Victorian three-storey block, turns the corner into Candleriggs.

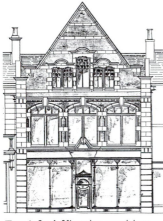

CDC Tech Services

Top left: A Victorian provisions store, Mill Street.
Top right: *The Cross,* junction of Mill Street and Mar Street, c. 1890.
Centre: Fusco's Cafe.
Above: The Hosiery.
Right: 41-45 Mill Street.

The name Shillinghill is derived from *sheiling* associated with hand threshing grain from the nearby corn mill, recollected by the title of one of the houses, Miller's House.

CDC Tech Services

The **Treetops Restaurant,** by J. M. Dick Peddie and George Washington Browne, 1906, was built as the British Linen Bank, and it shows: two-storey and attic red ashlar Jacobean facing Mill Street with pedimented doorways, balustrades above cornice at roofline, the Burgh Arms Shield and curvilinear gables; in short, Edwardian plush.

Mill Street continues with a row of two-storey shops and houses, with a staggered roofscape of slate, some roofs with dormers, most ending with straight skews or the solitary gable of crowsteps. **Paterson's Grain Store,** 1-3 Coalgate, is mid 18th century two-storey ashlar, with scrolled skewputts. This earlier building indicates where the new road abutted the original town, something the narrow angle of the older Coalgate emphasises. **5-11 Coalgate,** 1878, is a very busy mock baronial design by Adam Frame with scrolls, cornices and crowsteps.

CDC Tech Services

Treetops Restaurant.
Left: Chalmer's Church in 1856, note the thatched cottages and original Crown Hotel.

George Alexander Kerr
(1865-1927), a native of Lockerbie, and no relation to William, came to Alloa in 1893 and succeeded Leishman as Frame's assistant. In 1896 he established his own business, taking a partner, **William McCulloch,** from 1903, the partnership being dissolved on the latter's emigration in 1914. Kerr produced buildings of great quality, many with Art Nouveau detailing, the shop fronts of Fusco's Cafe, McEwan's and Whyte's still surviving.

CDC Libraries

Bank Street, developed after 1810, is the continuation of Mill Street into the West End, and the scale becomes grander, more suburban, and
18 establishment Victorian. Former **Chalmer's Church,** by John J. Murdoch and Wm. Hardie Hay of Liverpool, 1855-56, is characteristically original Gothic on a rectangular plan, the main feature the sturdy square tower, with diagonal buttressing to the corners, capped by a fine stone spire. Since the congregation united with St Andrew's (now North Church) in 1970, the church has been abused as a discotheque. **The Bruce Hotel,** c. 1870, formerly the

Below: Bank Street, the Bruce Hotel on the right.

Fowler

29

Fowler

Above: The Mercat Cross.
Right: The Burgh Chambers.

Thomas Frame & Son
Thomas Frame (1813-75), a native of Culross, settled in Alloa in 1852 as a joiner and builder. He was soon joined by his son Adam (1837-1901), who had trained as an architect, and they established the firm of Thomas Frame & Son.
Adam Frame had trained with Alexander (Greek) Thomson of Glasgow, Andrew Heiton of Perth, Murray Robertson in Dundee and William Railton in Kilmarnock. He was one of the few provincial architects to attempt to follow Alexander Thomson's idiosyncratic Egypto-Grecian. His major works were Alloa Burgh Chambers, the former Museum in Church Street and the finely detailed High Street/Mill Street corner block.
John Shaw Leishman
(1863-1908), younger son of an Alloa merchant, trained with Adam Frame and established his own firm c. 1893 in Alloa.

Crown, is an imposing two-storey hotel with twin projecting rectangular bays topped by classical hipped roofs, it looks like a squashed country house.

19 **Burgh Chambers,** Adam Frame, 1873-74
Splendidly ornate Victorian Renaissance facade, with rusticated ground floor, alternating pedimented upper floor and parapet. Nearly symmetrical, it has a rusticated pend arch to the west bay and, to the east a Corinthian columned porch, capped with a huge shield representing the Burgh Crest. On the first floor the bays continue with Corinthian pilasters, and end with balustraded parapets. The interior was reconstructed in 1907 after a fire: some interesting tile work, and fine panelling and plasterwork in the Council Chamber. Behind the pompous front block is a long row of primitive cells. Revitalised by the District Council, along with the **former Post Office and T.S.B.,** a poor continuation of the original by the same architect in 1882.

PSA

The Mercat Cross, Tobias Bauchop, 1690
Erected as a symbolic ornament by the 6th Earl of Mar in the Old Market Place (now Kilncraigs Mill entrance courtyard), and re-erected in front of the new Burgh Chambers. The restored mythical Griffin's head sits on an octagonal shaft.

Former **Commercial Bank,** 20-22 Bank Street,
David Rhind, 1848
Good banker's classical with fierce, quoinless
channelled stone ground floor and bracketed cornice at
roofline, by an architect who specialised in large
Italian palazzo-type banks. It is probably the building
that gave its name to the street. The quality of the Art
Nouveau frontage of **McEwan Decorators,** by
George Kerr, 1910, deserves notice.

Clydesdale Bank, 1852
More opulent banker's renaissance, ashlar stonework
channelled at street level, architraved windows above,
topped by a bracketed cornice. The corner doorpiece
is of granite Ionic columns, full entablature and
pediment, probably added by James Thomson of
Glasgow. The S.D.A. landscaped area beside the Bank
is **Meadow Place,** once more elegant, with fountain
and archways through to Coalgate. The building at
the Coalgate corner of Union Street, once part of
Younger's Brewery, has two re-used 18th century
stones built in (one with tailor's emblems), and huge
bargeboarded upper bow windows. The tall hipped
roofed tower behind was the Meadow Brewery malt
kiln.

20 **Gas Showrooms,** William Kerr, 1935-38
*A pleasing improvement to the architectural amenity of
one of the main entrances to Alloa* suggested the local
paper, referring to the frigid 1930s classical stone
frontage of showrooms and offices facing Bank Street,
with horizontal railings and Burgh Crest. The
remainder is a much more adventurous composition in
cream painted harling punctured by long strip
windows. The elevation to Coalgate contains flat-
roofed tiny shops, flanked by two huge cinemaesque
ovoid towers, massing to a central tower.

William Kerr (1866-1940), was
probably the most talented Alloa
architect. He became a partner in
John Melvin & Son in 1902 after
having served his apprenticeship
with Sir John James Burnet under
Alexander MacGibbon (1885-90),
and then being principal assistant
to Thomas Graham Abercrombie of
Paisley (1890-1902). A native of
Houston, he continued to live there
and commuted to Alloa by train.
Although most of Kerr's early
works in Alloa, like Kilncraigs
Offices and the Liberal Club, both
1904, are strictly classical, from his
arrival he was producing subtle
undecorated buildings using
powerful roof forms, and tall
Lutyenesque bay windows. These
include Sauchie Public Hall,
Paton's Sports Pavilion and the
Cochrane Hall in Alva. In the
1930s he produced buildings
comparable to those of any of the
young avant-garde architects. In
1912, he took a partner, **John
Gray,** to whom a share of the
credit for buildings attributed to
Kerr after this date must be given.
Kerr died in 1940 and in 1946 — a
few months before John Gray's
death — Gordon Biggar became a
partner. The firm was dissolved in
1985 on the latter's retiral.

Left: Gas Showrooms, Bank Street
facade.
Below: Coalgate elevation, from
Lime Tree Walk.

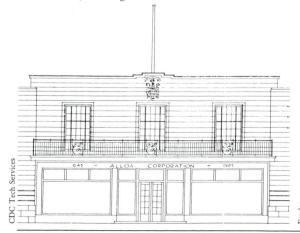

Fowler

21 **War Memorial,** Bank Street, Sir Robert Lorimer, 1923-24
The fine bronze of Britannia, surrounded by soldiers cutting barbed wire, was sculpted by C. d'O Pilkington Jackson, and is set in a landscaped stage flanked by a curved screen wall of stone.

Fowler

Mar Street (originally Cowie's Loan), was one of the streets laid out in the late 18th century improvements.
22 The **District Museum,** William Kerr, 1904, was built as the Liberal Club, in symmetrical Jacobean with a fine Doric-columned door. The main features are the windows: the first floor club rooms have tall mullioned oriel bays and the former billiard rooms above have sculpted dormers behind Art Nouveau balustrading, some with stained glass by Oscar Paterson. Part of the ground floor was retained by Kerr's firm, John Melvin and Son until 1985, as their own office with original screens, benches and other joiner work.

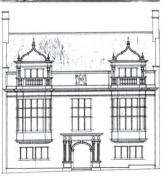

CDC Tech Services

23 **The District Library,** William Kerr, 1932
Converted from the Alloa Co-operative Society's headquarters, the facade is Thirties classical in red sandstone. Fluted pilasters flank the door with suitable date stones and emblems above.

19 Mar Street, c. 1825-30
A classical house of dressed stone, entered through a projecting pedimented central bay, between Ionic columns and under a fanlight. Behind is William Kerr's 1936 Y.M.C.A. hall building, in the pattern of large multi-paned windows, harled brick work, and low parapet walls which he developed for other local halls and schools at this time. The **Bank of Scotland,** 21 Mar Street, 1832, was built as a bank which may explain the use of the more solid Doric order for the columns.

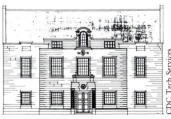

CDC Tech Services

Top: Candleriggs, looking up to Mar Street.
Centre: The District Museum.
Bottom: The District Library.

Alloa Advertiser, Arthur Bracewell, 1952
A 1950s facade in original condition, the stonework to
the ground floor elaborately curved with three doors
and two windows. A thin balcony runs along the
whole frontage, balustraded in wrought iron around
the central door.

The County and Police Buildings,
with the Sheriff Court fronting
Mar Street.
Below: 19 Mar Street.

24 **County and Police Buildings,** Brown and
Wardrop, 1863-64
Imposing Franco-Gothic, with crowstepped gablets,
and tall slender windows in ones, twos and threes. A
three-storey rectangular tower with a high French roof
marks the Drysdale Street corner. A matching
extension (1910) and Police Offices (1938) were added
by William Kerr.

25 **Ochil House,** mid-18th century
Originally the Plough Inn, converted in 1820 into a
Tontine Hotel, in 1844 into the County Offices; in
1882 the headquarters for volunteer army groups; in
the 1970s the social work department; and now, 200
years later, back into a hotel. Fairly expansive, two-
storey, entered through a projecting pedimented bay:
note the carving of a plough in the pediment.

26 **Mar Place House,** early 19th century
Set in a delightfully overgrown garden, almost hidden
from the busy roundabout which it faces, a simple
Georgian ashlar house with an Ionic columned door
and single-storey wings.

Moncrieff U.F. Church.

McLaren

27 **Moncrieff U.F. Church,** John Melvin, 1850
It is the gable that matters: huge with a crenellated parapet and pinnacled buttresses, enfolding a large traceried window flanked by narrow lancet windows. Original fittings inside include a horse-shoe gallery. Around the entrance are fine cast-iron balustraded steps. **Moncrieff House,** formerly the Manse, c. 1834, is a solid classical house with Doric door and hipped roof.

Former **County Offices,** 70 Drysdale Street, William Kerr, 1926
Imposing Jacobean, the symmetrical frontage reminiscent of the much earlier Liberal Club in Mar Street, with its heavy mullioned leaded windows. Above the simple door is the County motto *Look About Ye.*

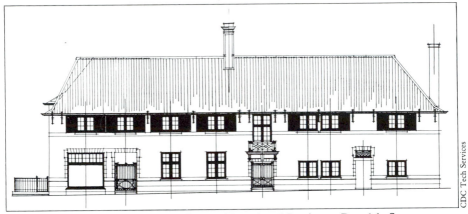

Townhead Institute.

CDC Tech Services

28 Former **Townhead Institute,** Drysdale Street, William Kerr, 1914
Arts and Crafts, in white harled brick under an immense swept roof. There are small horizontal windows with louvred shutters, high underneath the eaves. The large openings to Drysdale Street have plain stone mullions and date stones and upper windows open to a wrought-iron balustraded balcony. Built as Temperance Y.M.C.A. clubrooms (on the site of a popular hostelry — The Prince of Wales) by the paternalistic Forrester-Paton family.

High Street
Formerly High Coalgate, and now, with Mill Street, one of Alloa's principal commercial streets. The west side was rebuilt in the 1870s. **Nos. 8-16** form an interesting symmetrical range, a centred gable with rounded dormer wings, sadly out of scale with Adam Frame's neo-Greek building on the corner of Mill Street. Some original shopfronts survive, suggestive of the quality to which others could be restored.

George Brown (1818-1880), born in Alloa, founded the *Toronto Globe;* and later became Prime Minister of Upper Canada.

The east side of High Street escaped the Victorian but not modern development, and David MacGibbon's 1861 Scots baronial **National Bank** at the corner of Mill Street, was a particular loss. **The** 29 **Royal Bank of Scotland,** J. M. Dick Peddie, 1909, is an English baroque palace, with grand fluted Corinthian pilasters supporting an elaborate sculptured central pediment with the Bank's Arms.

Primrose Street
Once a residential street leading to the little valley of the Fairy Burn (on which first the Railway Station then the Leisure Centre was built), Primrose Street is now a mixture of shopfronts of different eras. The **Station Hotel** (once Victoria Hotel), 1886, is a rich building with an ornate moulded doorway, carved stone details and corner bay windows.

30 **Alloa Public Baths and Gymnasium,** Burnet and Campbell, 1895-98
Splendidly powerful Scots Renaissance, the elevation to Primrose Place is of particular quality. Although

Left: High Street, c. 1900.
Top: The Royal Bank of Scotland.
Above: Primrose Street retains the character shown in this 1894 drawing by Adam Frame.

Former Public Baths building.

partly modernised, there remains tilework, balustrading and sculpture of a strong Moorish character. The baths hall is not much altered from the Victorian period, when there were cubicles around the walls, potted palms, and trapezes swinging from the roof. It was presented to the town by John Thomson Paton of Kilncraigs Mill who also sponsored the Town Hall.

Bedford Place showing the former Burch School and the Parish Church: little has changed.

Alloa Glebe

The glebe, serving the former Manse at the head of Broad Street, stretched northwards from Bedford Place to Marshill. It was developed in the 1870s to form Ludgate Street, Coningsby Place, Glebe Terrace and Church Street: rows of Victorian villas many of which were designed by Adam Frame. Collectively interesting for their variety of large and small, single, double and flatted villas, with classical and Scots baronial features, **Birkendale**, 2-4 Coningsby Place, 1874, is notable: a double villa designed by Adam Frame, the western half for himself. The junction of Glebe Terrace and Coningsby Place forms an impressive piece of streetscape with the vast West End Park in the distance. The **West End Park,** opened in May 1878, was bought by the Burgh from the Earl of Mar and is entered through an impressive stone gateway from Grange Road.

31

Weir Pumps Social Club.

32 **Weir Pumps Social Club,** Church Street, Adam Frame, 1873
Built as the Library and Museum, it contains a hall behind a frigidly symmetrical facade — composed around a classical pediment propped up on four squat columns — of Alexander Thomson derivation.

Bedford Place and **Grange Road** formed a principal route west to Stirling, through spacious Regency and Victorian suburbs: **Nos. 9, 10, 12, 13 and 16** all date from about the year of Waterloo, classical villas in their own grounds overlooking the Forth, using the standard components of classical architecture — pilasters, columns, fanlights, architraves — to achieve individuality. **1 Bedford Place,** 1910, built as a garage and cycle shop for J. B. Whyte by George Kerr, retains its curved Art Nouveau windows. **The Royal Oak Hotel,** 1820s, in white painted ashlar, has unusual pilastered ends to the facade.

³³ **West Church,** Peddie and Kinnear, 1864
Gothic in style, with a rectangular plan, and tall campanile at the south-west corner, it was given Scots Gothic transepts, and a sanctuary in Oregon pine and marble by Sydney Mitchell and Wilson in 1902. The 1891 Church Hall was by Adam Frame. The nearby
³⁴ former **Burgh School,** by John Melvin, 1875, is elaborate Scots Baronial in style: a circular entrance tower with a conical roof, and crowstepped gable with a mullioned triple window, extended by George Kerr, 1910.

³⁵ **St Mungo's Parish Church,** James Gillespie Graham, 1817-19
Unusually delicate and picturesque for a Gillespie Graham unscholarly revival church. Usual symmetry in plan, but greater felicity than normal in lacy perpendicular Gothic; a 207 ft high spire with flying buttresses, topping a tower to the centre of the south

CDC Libraries

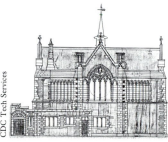

CDC Tech Services

Top: West Church.
Above: West Church additions, 1902: north elevation.

St Mungo's Parish Church.

Fowler

Robert Bald (1775-1861), son of the superintendent of the Alloa coal works, is remembered as the *enlightened mining engineer* of the Earls of Mar, who were extracting coal from Sauchie until the Alloa Coal Company was formed in 1844. Although, in 1832, he attributed miners' deaths from cholera to the *immoderate drinking of whisky*, he was a firm supporter of the Earl of Shaftesbury's Mines and Collieries Bill (1842), abolishing apprenticeship in mines, and excluding women and boys from working underground. Bald wrote: *A stout woman carried in general from a hundredweight to two hundredweight and in a trial of strength three hundredweight imperial. . . . It was not uncommon for the women ascending the stairs from the pit bottom to the surface to weep most bitterly from the severity of the labour.* One woman complained to him: *Oh sir, this is some work. I wish to God that the first woman who tried to bear coals had broken her back and none would have tried again.* Just prior to his death in 1861, Bald was recognised as having *rendered important services . . . throughout Europe, as a mining engineer* and had done much *to meliorate the condition of the mining population.* His brother **Alexander Bald** (1783-1859) ran the timber-yard and brick and tile works at Craigward, wrote a then indispensable book for Scottish tenant farmers, *The Corn Dealers Assistant,* and was a patron and friend to many literary figures, being among the first to acknowledge James Hogg, the Ettrick Shepherd.

Top right: Lylestone House.
Right: Stair mural.

frontage. Each corner of the church is graced with a low square tower with crenellated parapet. The spire is the precursor of Gillespie Graham's larger copy of Louth at Montrose. The interior and additions at the gables are by Leslie Graham MacDougall in Lorimer-derived Gothic. William Kerr added the classical Church Hall in 1926.

Fentoun House, 11 Bedford Place, c. 1840, is cut-stone classical, with fine moulded windows, architraves, pediments and a pilastered door: a 36 substantial stable block to the rear. **Bedford House,** 13 Bedford Place, c. 1855, is of similar proportions, but more ornate. Behind is **Bedford Court,** by Wheeler and Sproson, 1985, a Saltire Society award winning scheme of sheltered housing. **10 Bedford Place,** c. 1815, set in a walled garden, entered through rusticated gate piers and a Doric-columned doorway, faces south, originally overlooking the Forth. 37 Note the Venetian window. **Lylestone House,** 12 Bedford Place, 1815, is a fine, south-facing house with

elaborate windows on both facades, an Ionic-columned porch facing the street, a Doric one the garden. A circular, domed, stair is decorated with an unusual mural painting of Edinburgh from Fife, complete with steamboats. The house was home of the noted mining engineer, Robert Bald. **Westray,** next door, is contemporary, smaller and somewhat more delicate.

Grange Road continues Bedford Place, and **Nos. 1 and 2** date from c. 1830. Solid Doric doorpieces, ashlar stonework channelled at the ground level, and single-storey wings to each side. **3 Grange Road,** 1838, is a fine house with original window bars and 38 pilastered doorpiece. **The Old Rectory,** c. 1840, is a distinguished classical house, with a Doric-columned door, cornice, architraved windows, and well proportioned side wings. The octagonal chimney pots are worth a glance.

Left: 3 Grange Road.
Top: The Old Rectory.
Above: 38-50 Grant Street.

13 Grange Road, 1840s, has an ornamental pedestal at the centre, flanked by two bay windows; the entrance porch is in a wing to the east. Note the flower carving on the window lintels of **29-31 Grange Road,** 1870s, comparable to Adam Frame's Church Street Museum, implying a similar hand. **35-39 Grange Road,** 1880s, is a block of three plain houses unified by lovely wrought-iron door pediments. **40 Grange Road,** another 1830s villa, has its back to the main road and another fine Doric-columned door.

39 **St John's Primary School,** Grant Street, William Kerr, 1902, is a red brick courtyard in what became Kerr's usual style with large multi-paned windows, 40 green slate roof and belfry. **38-50 Grant Street** are 1903 workers' housing by Sir John Burnet in the Arts and Crafts manner: square brick columns, wooden porch lintels and long rows of dormers.

John's Primary School.

Above: A 1910 cottage by William Kerr now marooned between the railway line and Stirling Road.
Right: Grange School.

41 **Grange School,** Grange Road, George A. Kerr, 1908
Art Nouveau in red sandstone, the block is symmetrical with two huge gabled bays, with Art Nouveau lettering at first floor level. The rooms are planned around a galleried centre hall, and Kerr expressed his Christian ideals with improving inscriptions such as *Study to show thyself approved unto God,* and a tiled dado of Christian symbols around the hall.

42 **Cowdenpark,** Stirling Road, John Melvin, 1850
A Tudor-Jacobean mansion built for Alexander Paton of Kilncraigs Mill, with a harled gabled frontage, with strong horizontal string courses exaggerated into architraves around the window heads. The nearby **Lodge,** and the lodge at Claremont, belonged to John
43 Thomson Paton's splendid mansion, **Norwood,** by John Melvin, 1874.

Below: Cowdenpark.
Right: Original drawing.

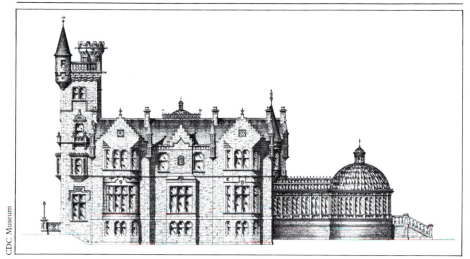

Arnsbrae House, Stirling Road, Alfred Waterhouse 1885, extended by Paul Waterhouse
Hiding behind trees, this red rubble, gabled mansion has a Gothic doorway, an arched loggia and an elegant terrace. The 1885 stable block has been converted into housing. The **Lodge** is a T-plan cottage with half timbered gables and decorative ridges.

Above: Norwood House (demolished).
Below: Arnsbrae House.

Marshill
Alloa Town Hall, Alfred and Paul Waterhouse, 1888
Its huge entrance gable, with a large arched doorpiece and curvilinear gable, dominates the Ring Road. The Hall has many fine architectural details, including Ionic pilasters, chimney, and a marvellously tiled staircase. The Hall, which included Alloa's first public library, was donated by John Thomson Paton of Norwood whose sculpted bust sits in the entrance hall. The townspeople had to contribute towards the library running costs in their rates. In the two-storey

Patons
Paton is a name long associated with the district. James Paton of Balliliesk, Muckhart, was ordained as Bishop of Dunkeld in 1572, later to be dismissed for having *no function or charge in the Reformed Kirk.* About 1760 James and Andrew Paton left Muckhart to become weavers and dyers in Alloa. James' son, John Paton (1768-1848), established the successful Kilncraigs spinning mill, made famous by his descendants. His elder sons, James (1797-1882) and David (d. 1891), founded their own textile mill at Tillicoultry, long continued by James' family. Kilncraigs passed to John Paton's daughters, for his third son Alexander (of Cowdenpark) died without a successor in 1860. John Thomson Paton (1831-1910) of Norwood, donor of the Town Hall and Public Baths, and David Thomson (1853-1917) of Greenfield House, were sons of the eldest daughter. Mary (d. 1881), the youngest Paton daughter, founded the Forrester-Paton family, exponent of the Temperance Movement, and great patrons of Alloa, latterly of Inglewood and The Gean.

41

Fowler

CDC Libraries

Above: Alloa Town Hall.
Right: Contemporary engraving.

roofspace were built well-lit science rooms and art studios for the benefit of the town.

44 **Marshill House** and **6 Marshill** are two more of
45 Alloa's early 19th century classical villas both of which have good columned porches and fine marble, plasterwork, and fireplaces inside.

46 **The South African War Memorial,** Robert Lorimer, 1904
Quietly forgotten within the verdant shrubberies of a peaceful memorial garden, the relocated monument was sculpted to Lorimer's design by W. B. Birnie Rhind: a Highlander, with his hand on his revolver, standing over a wounded colleague.

OPPOSITE
Top right: Craigmyle.
Centre: Struan House.
Below left: Claremont House.
Below right: Fish gargoyle, Claremont House.

Kellie Place has a number of late Victorian Scots villas by John Melvin. The **Endrick Hotel** and its neighbouring twin, c. 1880, are large detached villas with Franco-Gothic towers echoing that of the County Buildings.

Claremont was the old road from Alloa to Stirling, *a quiet rural road,* until it was developed for large villas after the railway bridge was built at Marshill in 1851. The villas on the north side of Claremont are modest and most were built at the turn of the century. George Kerr intended **No. 38,** 1898, half of a double villa, to be his own home, but was unable to move owing to
47 illness. **No. 30,** probably by Adam Frame, c. 1900, is a modest villa, its Egyptian door columns showing the continuing influence of Alexander (Greek) Thomson.
  The houses on the south side are much grander. **Claremont Grove (No. 21),** is a vast Georgianised house with a 1913 west wing by William Kerr. **No. 31,** 1902, was designed by William McCulloch (later to become George Kerr's partner), a plain Victorian

corner mansion, more typical of Glasgow dormitory
towns.

48 **Struan House (No. 33),** by William Kerr, 1905, is
a white harled L-plan house and not unlike
contemporary houses by Charles Rennie Mackintosh.

Craigmyle by John Melvin, 1902, has a very steep
hipped roof, canted bay windows to the south, and a
three-storey round tower. There is the unmistakable
hand of William Kerr in the detailing of the columned
porch.

Craig-na-Aird (No. 37), 1902, and **Claremont**
49 **House (No. 39),** 1901, were both by Melvin, the
latter being very similar to Craigmyle, but on a larger
scale. It was built as the Parish Manse, and is now the
home of the Earl of Mar and Kellie. The ornamental
features include rainwater heads in the form of fish.

Claremont has expanded westwards along both sides
of the ridge, comprising 1930s bungalows, more
recent speculative housing estates, and the vast **Alloa
Academy** complex, County Architect, 1957 onwards.

The Gean.

McLaren

Below: A drawing room at the Gean.
Below right: The Hall, Inglewood.

RCAHMS

The Gean, between Claremont and Tullibody Road, William Kerr, 1912
One of Kerr's finest buildings, the Gean is a large English mansion house clearly influenced by Sir Edwin Lutyens, set in vast grounds. Mullioned and transomed windows, a high, red-tile roof with tiny dormer windows, large gables and chimneys, a tower and classical porch, are matched by equal splendour inside: carved panelling, balustrading and plasterwork. It was built for Alexander Forrester-Paton as a wedding present from his parents. The house and lodges require attention if they are to survive.

Inglewood, Tullibody Road, A. G. Sydney Mitchell and Wilson, 1900

RCAHMS

James Sligo Jameson
(1856-1888), an intrepid naturalist and South African explorer, was born at the Walk House, Limetree Walk. His family had been Sheriff Clerks since 1765. Aged 21, James visited Borneo to collect wildlife specimens; later, the Kalahari Desert to hunt big game, and then on to explore Kipling's *great grey-green, greasy Limpopo River*. Trips to the Rocky Mountains, Spain and Algeria followed. In 1887 he joined H. M. Stanley's controversial Congo expedition as a naturalist, from where he sent home authoritative papers, before succumbing to a fever.

A huge symmetrical Jacobean house. The south frontage has two-storey bay windows with verandah, rising to huge curve and triangular shaped gables. A four-storey tower rises to the south-east and to the north is a Doric-columned porch. Rich plasterwork and panelling inside, with glasswork by Oscar Paterson. The **East Lodge** and **Stables,** now the **Coach House Theatre,** have similar features to the main house. The **West Lodge** is smaller, half-timbered to the road, with a canted bay to the drive. The gateway has half-rusticated piers, arched footgates and urn finials.

50 **Paton and Baldwin's Sports Pavilion,** Tullibody Road, William Kerr, 1926
Wide overhanging, red-tiled roof, with hipped roof wings to the either side, shelters facades of white-painted, harled brickwork, punctured by horizontal windows along the roof line and a low glazed verandah between the wings. To either side of the wings are bell-roofed octagonal towers, and in the centre of the main roof ridge is an imposing clock turret.

Top: Inglewood, c. 1905.
Above: The East Lodge and Stables, Inglewood.

51 **Alloa North Church,** Ludgate, Adam Frame, 1882
Built as St Andrew's Parish Church on the site of the Ludgate, or Round Toll. Contemporaries admired *the massive appearance emphasised by the bold proportions of the buttresses and deep splays on the window jambs and the high pitch of the roof.* **Alloa Baptist Church,** opposite, is a simple 1882 rectangle in a *modified Gothic style* by James Mitchell.

52 **District Council Headquarters,** Greenfield House, A. G. Sidney Mitchell and Wilson, 1892-94
Set in flat, well-treed parkland, Greenfield is a good

Greenfield House, drawn by Alex Brown.

Greenfield House.

example of the red sandstone aspirations of a rich merchant, who went to Edinburgh for the most fashionable architects of the day. Thomson Paton wealth purchased a great towered confection complete with look-out tower, two-storey bay windows and tall chimneys. Reconstructed and extended by the same architects after a 1914 fire, many original fittings remain — including fine wood panelling and plasterwork — particularly in the Council Chamber. It was bought by the Town Council in 1952 and is now the principal offices of the District Council, its grounds a public park. Recently extended sympathetically to the rear by District Council Architects.

54 **Alloa Co-operative Sports Pavilion,** Sunnyside Road, George Kerr, 1925
A handsome cream coloured Pavilion in the Scots domestic style, it faces west, with little hipped roof towers at the corners, portico, verandah and balcony.

Alloa Co-operative Sports Pavilion.

55 **Clackmannan County Hospital,** Ashley Terrace, R. A. Bryden (of Clarke & Bell, Glasgow), 1897-99
A cottage hospital sponsored by Miss C. Forrester-Paton, fronting the original Alloa Hospital which had been built in 1868 (the year cutlasses were first issued to the Burgh Police Force).

56 **Sunnyside Primary School,** Erskine Street, John Bennie Wilson, 1892
An imposing symmetrical red and grey stone Board

School, of classrooms around a tiled hall and gallery above. Inscribed pediments and neat twin belfries.

Clackmannan Road is the main thoroughfare
57 heading east from Alloa Town Centre. **Park Villas** were built from 1872 by local builders and joiners, soon followed by Park Place.

Hawkhill
58 The local authority housing on the south side dates from 1948. One half of a double-house celebrates its private ownership with stone applied over the render. The little side porches to these houses have modernist aspirations. A little scheme of attractive cottage housing by the District Council, 1986, is hidden behind the earlier scheme.

Cross Slab, Hawkhill
An early Christian standing stone, with a rough incised cross to either side, lies to the south of the road, between Alloa and Clackmannan.

Whins Road
59 **Alloa Brewery** was established on its present site in 1810 but the present complex is modern. The Brewery car park was the site of Thomson Brothers **Springfield Mill,** a spinning and carding factory founded in 1844, and burnt c. 1901. **Gaberston** was another Victorian Mill, producing tartan shawls, plaids, and handkerchiefs for David Lambert from 1837. Gaberston Farm and Gaberston House are reminders that this was once a rural area.
60 **Carsebridge Distillery** founded by John Bald in 1799, recently closed. **Carsebridge House** is a sturdy, Victorianised, late 18th century dwelling, with a walled garden containing a Doric column looted in Egypt by Napoleon.

Swan

Below: The Napoleon Pillar.
Below left: Clackmannan County Hospital.

CDC Tech Services

The Napoleon Pillar
A Doric column dating from Roman occupation of Egypt. Its inscription reads:

This Pillar was conquest of Napoleon at Grand Cairo in Egypt in the year 1798
and
having been captured by the Allies en route to France
was sent by them to Florence
where it was bought by my father C. E. DEDE
and forwarded to
Altona Schleswig Holstein
Fraulein Dede, Altona den 14 ten August 1852
Above Pillar presented by J. B. Harvey
by Mrs Dede.

OLD SAUCHIE

The Schaws of Sauchie

Sauchie was granted to Henri de Annand, kinsman to King Robert Bruce, in 1321, passing into the Schaw family a century later. The Schaws of Sauchie were among the most influential families of mediaeval Scotland. Sir James Schaw, Governor of Stirling Castle, refused James III access to his son, and thus played a major role in the conspiracy that led to the king's murder at Sauchieburn in 1488. George Schaw, Abbot of Paisley, was Lord High Treasurer of Scotland in 1495 and the Schaws continued as Governors of Stirling Castle to James IV. The Schaw crest of three covered golden cups commemorates the hereditary post of Master of the Royal Wine Cellar granted to Alexander Schaw in 1529, and reconfirmed on his grandson by James VI. William Schaw (1550-1602), was king's *Master of Work* responsible for work at Stirling Castle, Holyrood and Dunfermline Abbey and for developing Freemasonry in Scotland. The Sauchie lands fell to a kinsman after George Schaw died without heir about 1690, and then passed, by his daughter's marriage in 1752, to the Cathcart family. William Schaw Cathcart, the first Earl (1755-1843), was the most distinguished of a remarkable family of statesmen. As Russian Ambassador, his services were *of the greatest importance in the overthrow of Napoleon.* He retired to Britain, but sold Schawpark to his sister's family, Earls of Mansfield, in 1826. The house, offices and grounds still conveyed *the idea of decayed grandeur* in the mid 19th century, but was unroofed in 1925 and finally demolished in the 1950s.

Fowler

SAUCHIE

Old Sauchie (place of the willows) grew up around the old Tower on the northern slopes of the Devon valley. But, as the later Sauchie landlords — Schaws and Cathcarts — prospered as mineowners, their estate workers became miners and the settlement moved south to the mines, leaving the Tower almost isolated. Circa 1700 the Schaw family moved to their mansion of Schawpark by Gartmorn, the mining village near them becoming Newtonschaw. The Earl of Mar's miners' cottages at Holton Square was the first of many colliery rows in the area, and by the mid-19th century — with the collected mining villages becoming *New Sauchie* — almost a suburb of Alloa.

Sauchie Tower, c. 1430

On a fine site with spectacular views north over the Devon to the Ochils, Sauchie owes its survival to fashion: the fashion that led the Schaws to abandon the Tower for a new mansion house within the enclosure in 1631; and again to quit that mansion for their splendid seat of Schawpark near Fishcross, some 70 years later. Both mansions are demolished, to the District's grievous loss, but the Tower is subject to promising restoration plans by Bob Heath.

Begun by Sir James Schaw, whose family had come from Greenock 100 years earlier to marry the daughter of Henri de Annand of Sauchie, the Tower is built of beautifully squared blocks of pink sandstone (itself an

Above: Sauchie Tower.

unusual sign of quality shared with Clackmannan), and stands to four storeys with cap-house. Remains of outer fortifications are clearly visible and await excavation. Defensive features on the Tower include a parapet walk with roundels in the corners, corbelled out on machicolations for the deterrence of strangers below. As usual, the principal internal room is on the first floor, with bedrooms above; and some rooms are within the wall thickness. The vaulted ground floor cellar has an unusual entresol fitted in beneath the vault, as a later private room. The hall above contains a grand fireplace with finely sculpted jambs, windows with stone benches, and a stone wash basin with a carved Gothic head.

In addition to manufacturing Osnaburgh (coarse linen originally from Germany) at Sauchie, Lord Cathcart encouraged the weaving of camblets (woollen garments). In 1775, Lord Cathcart, who had inherited Schawpark, planned to have the house remodelled by Robert Adam, but died before the full plans could be implemented; and what was achieved, with its odd Gothic gables and windows, to a most unusual plan, was demolished in the 1950s.

RCAHMS

RCAHMS

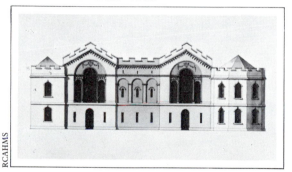

RCAHMS

Top: Sauchie Tower.
Above: Old Sauchie House.
Left: Schawpark north front, Robert Adam's 1775 drawing.
Below: The Cathcart family, Schawpark, by David Allan 1784; commemorating the first cricket match held in Scotland.

Royal Academy of Arts/Earl of Cathcart

In 1760, Bishop Pococke of Meath visited Schawpark, *we went to Lord Cathcart's, on a rising ground about a mile from the mountains. The approach to it is round three sides of the plantations, and by a Village partly new built, where the present Lord has settled a Manufacture of Osnaburgs. Half a mile further stands the house of a very singular form. . . .* Pococke then describes the house with its bow windows, battlements, cornice, pediments, balcony and square towers and the gardens surrounding the house.

Auchinbaird Windmill.

61 **Auchinbaird Windmill,** early 18th century
Originally built to harness wind power to the draining of a coal pit, it was converted into a dovecot at the pit's closure: a rubble-built, circular tower with domed roof and castellated parapet, much the worse of time.

Devon Village, mid-19th century
A simple row of little-altered charming cottages. The 62 **Devon Colliery Beam Engine House,** 1865, is a tall, rectangular ashlar building of high quality workmanship, with arched openings and hipped slate roof. The engine, a Cornish Pumping Engine to drain the mine shaft, was built by Neilson & Co. of Glasgow. The cast-iron beam and pump have survived, but the remainder was removed for scrap metal. The only other beam pumping engine in Scotland survives at Prestongrange, East Lothian, in the working museum.

Fishcross
Originally an 18th century miners' row where the Sheardale Ridge road crossed that between Alloa and Tillicoultry, part of which still remains along the north side of Pitfairn Road. The **Primary School and Schoolhouse,** Adam Frame, 1887, are Gothic. **The Miners' Welfare Institute,** William Kerr, 1930, is very similar to Sauchie Public Hall but on a smaller scale. It has Kerr's hallmarks of large bay windows and steep overhanging pitched roofs.

Devon Colliery Beam Engine House.

The **Devon Iron Works** were begun in 1792 by the Devon Company to exploit the rich seams of coal and limestone on Lord Cathcart's estate of Sauchie. Two 40 ft high furnaces were built into a cliff above the Devon, just to the east of Sauchie Tower. The quarry face also supported the casting house and furnace air pump engine house. Iron ore was imported and manufactured goods exported through Alloa. By 1842, ironstone was being obtained locally, whilst limestone was brought from South Queensferry. After a third furnace was built, the works produced about 6,000 tons of pig-iron per annum, for the foundry which turned them into cast-iron goods for sale. The Works closed in 1856.

Fowler

Gartmorn Dam, 1713 onwards
The oldest, and for many years the largest, man-made reservoir in Scotland, built by the Earl of Mar to provide water power via a lade, to drain his coal mines at Holton.

63 An **Information and Interpretative Centre** was created out of the former Pump House by the District Council Architects in 1982 and provides exhibition facilities relevant to the Country Park and to the Countryside Ranger Service based at the Dam. Leaflet to Gartmorn Dam Country Park available.

New Sauchie
It is difficult to pinpoint a centre for this community as it bestrides the route from Alloa northwards. **Main Street,** having accordingly suffered the usual road widening, may have lost whatever sense of containment it once had. **Sauchie Drill Hall,** built in 1819 as the Holton School, provides Sauchie with a prominent landmark with its square castellated tower.

A former resident of Holton Square described her single end (one room house) to Ian Adamson: *The room was very small and had a stone floor. Behind the door was a large shelf arrangement and taking up most of one wall, was a range which, in these days, served as a cooker, clothes dryer for wet working clothes and room heater. Two double beds occupied most of the floor area, one was for the six children and the other was for the parents. There was little room for much else in the way of furniture than a wardrobe or dresser and of course a po' under the bed as there was no toilet or even running water in the house.*

Left: Information Centre, Gartmorn Dam.

Gartmorn provided the water that eventually gave Alloa the power for its industrialisation. A four-mile lade was constructed to bring water westwards to flood the marshy hollow of Gartmorn from the River Black Devon at Forestmill. The earthen dam has been rebuilt, and until recently, the 162-acre reservoir has provided Alloa, local breweries and distilleries with fresh water. The Gartmorn Country Park was recognised as a Local Nature Reserve in 1980, for the 215-acre estate is an important nesting and wintering site for many species of wild fowl.

New Sauchie.

Fowler

Top: Main Street before
redevelopment.
Above: Sauchie Parish Church.

Sauchie Public Hall.

Holton Cottages, Burnbrae
The original miners' row lies on the east as Main
64 Street turns the corner uphill. **Keilarsbrae House,**
c. 1830, currently being restored, is another good
classical villa of the sort in western Alloa; well-cut
stonework, a doorway aggrandised by Doric pilasters,
and a fine wrought-iron staircase inside. **Craigbank** is
an excellent 1950s scheme of terraces and low flats in
brick with fashionable horizontal windows, portholes
65 and door details. The Gothic **Sauchie Parish
Church,** 1841-42, is designed to exploit its
commanding site with a tall square tower at the east
end, and a parapeted pinnacled roof. Excellent internal
woodwork. The adjacent **Manse** is 1872. **Greycraigs
House,** mid-19th century, is similar to Keilarsbrae,
even though some 20 years younger.

66 **Sauchie Public Hall,** Fairfield Road, William Kerr,
1911, extended 1925
A jewel-like, red and white, Arts and Crafts hall,
distinguished by its colour, overhanging steep-pitched
roof, large multi-pane bay windows, leaded lights,
recessed archway and buttresses — this is one of
Kerr's best buildings, currently undergoing a
renaissance.

Former **Sauchie School,** Mar Place, 1887, was built by Adam Frame in uneventful Gothic, on the site of the Equity Court House (or *Ha'house*), established in 1765 as a Bailie Court by the Erskines to settle disputes of the Holton mineworkers. Its environs have now been greatly improved by S.D.A. Land Renewal.

[67]The **U.F. Church,** by John Bruce, 1932, is a simple harled brick church with reconstituted stone dressings, signalled by its imposing square clock tower.

Tullibody Auld Kirk.

Fowler

TULLIBODY

Strategically positioned where the River Devon curves to meet the Forth at Cambus, Tullibody was the site of Kenneth McAlpine's camp preceding his battle with the Picts near Cambuskenneth in A.D. 834, which led to the uniting of the Kingdoms of the Scots and the Picts. After winning, Kenneth returned to Tullibody and erected a stone pillar as a memorial. In 1643, on the eve of his march to the battle of Kilsyth, the Marquis of Montrose quartered his men in Tullibody Woods, and while he dined with the Earl of Mar, his men *barbarously plundered* Alloa.

Circa 1800, the original Clachan nestling around the Auld Kirk was removed, and the Abercromby laird laid out a new settlement on village riggs to the south. These new houses were in the area around Main Street, but most have subsequently been demolished. In the late 19th century, the village expanded with the arrival of the tannery, and again in the 1950s when the Scottish Special Housing Association and the County Council provided houses for the new miners.

[68]**Auld Kirk,** Menstrie Road, 16th century
Little visible in the roofless remains can be traced to

To the north of Tullibody Auld Kirk lie the remains of a stone coffin known as The Maiden Stone. Around 1450 the priest of Tullibody is said to have deceived Martha Wishart, the Maid of Myretoun, as to his intentions. On her death bed, she instructed that her body was to be placed in a raised coffin by the church door, to shame the irreverent priest. The priest must have suffered, for he had the church door changed from the north to the south side.

Tullibody has its place in the history of the Reformation. Thomas Cocklaw, the last priest of the Catholic persuasion, adopted the principles of the reformers. On finding marriage warranted by the Scriptures, he took himself a wife, but the clergy retaliated by putting the attendants at his wedding to death. Cocklaw escaped with the Canon of Cambuskenneth to sanctuary in England: we are not told of the fate of his new wife.

Top: Abercromby Memorial, Auld Kirk.
Above: St Serf's Parish Church.

Tullibody School was famed for the high quality of its teachers, encouraged by the Lairds. In 1794, Sir Ralph Abercromby wrote from Antwerp that a new school and schoolhouse be built. The schoolmaster of the time, Alexander Seggie, was so renowned a classical scholar that more young men from this school went to colleges than from the rest of the schools in Clackmannanshire put together.

1149 when David I granted the Lands and Inches of Tullibody to Cambuskenneth Abbey. The remains are those of a rectangular 16th century building which, after its destruction by the French army of Mary of Guise in 1559, fell into disrepair. Restored and re-roofed by George Abercromby in 1760, and presented with a bellcote and an old Man-of-War ship's bell, and again restored in 1833, it was abandoned in 1904 as unsafe. Some fine memorials include the Corinthian pilastered frame which once contained a tribute to the first laird, George Abercromby (d. 1699), from Alexander Abercromby whom he adopted as his heir. The kirkyard includes interesting 18th century monuments, and an unsual 1830 cast-iron memorial to James Donaldson of the Devon Ironworks.

St Serf's Parish Church, Peter MacGregor Chalmers, 1904
Charmingly simple Romanesque with circular piers in the north aisle, this little church is set back on a grassy knoll overlooking the Devon Valley. Rubble stonework throughout. The 1837 bell at the front came from the Auld Kirk. The **Church Hall,** by John Burnet, 1844, was built as Tullibody's Free Church to *a superior design to many buildings for a similar object in this quarter* in pointed Gothic. One of the earliest surviving buildings of John Burnet senior, it was converted into the Church Hall in 1951. The 1847 **Manse** adjacent is sternly classical.

69 **The Tannery,** Alloa Road, 1880, founded by Alexander Paterson, c. 1806
A large two-storey red-brick block with windows picked out in white brick, is capped by a further two storeys of windows and louvred timber ventilators, for through draughts and dissipation of stench. Founded by a shoemaker desiring to tan his own leather, it became the largest tannery in Scotland, dominated by its top-heavy brick water tower. It took its water from the Delph Pond, historically the common property of the village. Now converted to a plastics factory, with significant tanning relics inside.

Main Street
The heart of planned Tullibody lay south of Alloa Road, represented by a Main Street straddling the route to Cambus. Not much of historic interest remains in Main Street, the present centre of the village being Tron Court, a shopping precinct designed by W. H. Henry, County Architect, in 1967, to replace decaying cottages. A number of attractive 19th century houses and cottages in **Delph Road** are the sole survivors of the 19th century village: **No. 11** is a picturesque harled and pantiled cottage with its

Tullis

own stable and **No. 4** is a simple classical house. The **Tron Tree,** a lime planted by the village well, marked the location of the public weighing machine.

School Road

Cambus and Tullibody Institute, 1904, George Kerr, is a Gothic village hall, with Arts and Crafts buttresses, and the hopeful motto over the door: *Let there be light:* there was light! **Abercromby School,** W. H. Henry (County Architect), 1951, was the first post-war community school in the County, more like a village college: comprising a maternity and child welfare clinic, adult education provision, and the primary school. The assembly hall block is an exercise in bare geometrics. **The Nursery,** by Central Region Architects, 1984, takes the form of a glass-clad steel pyramid.

Tullis

Above: The Tannery and Delph Pond, and the tannery workings, c. 1910.
Below left: Main Street.
Below: The Nursery.

Swan

Fowler

The Lych Gate.

Swan

Robert Dick (1811-1866) was a native of Tullibody, his father an exciseman at Cambus and later Dall's Distillery, Glenochil. All his adult life he worked in poverty as a baker in Thurso, to support his studies into the natural sciences of the Caithness District. Hugh Miller, who received many geological and botanic specimens from Dick, wrote that *he has robbed himself to do me service.*

The Lych Gate and War Memorial, 1921
Built at the entrance to Tullibody Park and now lacking its inscribed panels. A large boulder known as *Samson's Button* or the *Haer Stane,* was utilised as its base, into which was plugged a replica of the *Standin' Stane of Kenneth McAlpine* — destroyed in 1806.

70 **Baingle Brae,** Alexander Taylor, 1834 (demolished)
This very fine Hamiltonesque towered villa was built by Alexander Paterson of the Tannery following a trip to Italy. Perhaps some Palladian country villa inspired the tall glass cupola and formal gardens. The seven acres of gardens, renowned for their beauty, were lost with the house to the excited housing programme of the 1960s.

Baingle Brae.

RCAHMS

RCAHMS

Tullibody House, c. 1710 (demolished)

Tullibody House, which used to exist on a
magnificent site by the shore, was the paternal seat of
the Abercromby family, who later moved to Airthrey.
It was a tall, old Scots house, plain and well ordered
under its steep, hipped roof. Its grounds were
constantly being improved according to the fashion of
the time. George Abercromby was a leader in

Tullibody House.

Tullibody House

*The old house of Tullibody was built
a few years before the Restoration by
Mr Robert Meldrum. In point of
shape it resembled the old house of
Newton, being only larger. Mr
Abercromby remembers it before his
father demolished it to build the
present house, which he set down in a
corn ridge. His fir woods, taken off
the moor, were enclosed and planted
between 1725 and 1753. In 1750
Tullibody was one of the neatest and
best places in the country. It was, no
doubt, in the very reverse of the
present airy style. If, however,
avenues and clipped hedges conveyed
an idea of formality and constraint,
they afforded shade and shelter both
in heat and cold. And they were
commonly disposed either to set
capital objects in a striking point of
view or to hide deformities. . . .
Perhaps I am partial to the place
where I spent many of the happiest
days of my youth — where I learned
what no books can teach and where I
formed my earliest friendships and
views of life.* John Ramsay.

University of Dundee

Sir Ralph Abercromby's son James
(1776-1858), the future judge Lord
Dunfermline, by David Allan 1779.

TULLIBODY HOUSE

The Abercrombies came to Clackmannanshire from Skein in Aberdeenshire, George (d. 1699) buying the estate c. 1655. Alexander (1675-1754), the second laird, was only a near relative who had lived with George since childhood. A committed Hanoverian, he built the house and laid out the grounds, acquiring Menstrie Castle in 1719. His son, George (1705-1800), second of Tullibody, one-time Professor of Law at Edinburgh University, was the laird who brought fame to the estate. A noted improver, he lived to the age of 95: to see his first son knighted, Sir Ralph Abercromby, later hero of the battle of Aboukir Bay in which he was killed; his second son knighted, Sir Robert Abercromby, Governor of Bombay; and his third son Lord Abercromby, a Law Lord in the Court of Session.

In *Waverley* Sir Walter Scott relates how his young hero Edward Waverley, a guest at Tully-Veolan House, pays a visit to an outlawed clan chieftain — Donald Bean Lean — to negotiate the return of his host's stolen cattle. The story was based on an incident when, as a young man, Abercromby found that his cattle were apt to disappear, stolen by raiders of the Clan MacGregor. Abercromby chose to visit the celebrated Rob Roy MacGregor, and it is this visit to Rob Roy's cave that is recounted by Scott. *Mr Abercromby was regaled with collops from two of his own cattle, and was dismissed in perfect safety, after having agreed to pay in future a small sum of blackmail, in consideration of which Rob Roy not only undertook to forbear his herds in future but to replace any that should be stolen from him by other freebooters.*

agricultural improvement and a founder of the Highland Society in 1784. In the 19th century, the setting of the house became increasingly industrialised (something the Abercrombies might have seen as progress) and it was demolished in the early 1960s as a result of railway works and vandalism.

Tullibody Old Bridge, Bridgend, Stirling Road, c. 1535 and 1697
Unusually long, 442 ft, and varying in width from 20 ft down to 11½ ft, the bridge has two principal arches

over the river and (as the Devon is prone to flooding at this point) three flood arches to the west. At the main crossing point of the River Devon, this bridge had its eastern arch broken down by Kirkcaldy of Grange in 1559. It had been one of several bridges erected in the neighbourhood of Stirling by Robert Spittal, philanthropist and Royal tailor (see *Stirling and the Trossachs*).

71 **Doocot,** New Mills Crossing, 17th century
A lean-to Doocot in a sad state of repair, with crumbling crowstepped walls containing a fair number of nesting boxes.

Swan

Cambus

The village of Cambus (a creek or haven) is situated at the confluence of the River Devon with the Forth. A dam was built on the Devon to drive corn and barley mills on each side of the river, and a pier was built to allow flat-bottomed boats to deliver and receive the grain and flour. For years there was a flourishing salmon industry based at Cambus, but declined owing to the pollution of the two rivers. Beer had been brewed at Cambus for centuries before Robert Knox

Swan

Tullibody was seen by contemporaries as a centre of enlightenment and intelligence in an arcadian setting. Witness the memory of John Ramsay of Ochertyre who referred to it as the *loved haunt of my youth*. He visited it again, as an old man in 1803: *I was glad to see the house so much improved, yet so much like what it was in the cheerful morn of my youth.* In 1809, he recorded after another visit: *Our entertainment was good but not overloaded or overdressed, and I have seldom seen a second course more honoured in the eating. Even I ate some fritters not to be particular . . . the conversation was very good . . . the house is a good one and much improved and without doors everything is gay and well disposed. Plenty of gravel walks and good roads. . . .*

In 1697, John, 6th Earl of Mar agreed with Mason Thomas Bauchop (father of the more famous Alloa Master Mason Tobias Bauchop, who witnessed the document) that *the said Thomas shall construct and build a new arch at the east end of the bridge of Tullibody, finish the gate, and mend the pear of the mid pillars thereof, and to bat it with iron, mend the calsie of the whole bridge, and to put on a tirlace gate, with lock and key thereto. . . .* It is uncertain how much of the present structure was Spittal's bridge and how much Bauchop's.

After Kirkcaldy of Grange had broken down the bridge to retard the process of the Queen Regent's French Army, the latter improvised with the now Protestant Kirk roof instead. According to John Knox: *The French, expert anouch sicne factis, tuik don the roofe of a parish church and maid a brig over the watter called Dovane and so they aschapit and came to Striveling, and syne to Leith.*

Above: New Mills Doocot.
Left: Cambus.

Cast Iron Bridge, Cambus.
Right: Cambus Distillery.

King O'Muirs is associated with
James V who, in one of his
wanderings incognito as the
Gudeman of Ballengeich, was
offered hospitality by one
Donaldson, then tenant.
Ballengeich suggested that
Donaldson might visit him at
Stirling Castle, where he
discovered his guest to have been
the king. The king presented
Donaldson with the title *King of
the Muirs.* The last Donaldson of
King O'Muirs moved to Alloa,
where it is said that King Street
was named after him.

In 1814, twenty *ca'ing* whales
swam aground at Cambus and were
killed. James Hogg immortalised
the tragedy thus:

*Ane hundred and threttye bordlyie
   whailis
Want snorying up the tydde.
And wyde on Allowais fertylle holmis
They gallopit ashore and died.*

established his brewery in 1786, but Cambus is
probably more noted for its **Distillery** and bonding
sheds, founded in 1806 by John Moubray. The 19th
century distillery was burnt down in 1914 and totally
rebuilt in 1937. Only part of the **Still House Tower**
remained to give the present building some connection
with the past. There is a fine example of an early 19th
century cast iron **Bridge** leading from the Distillery
to the east bank of the Devon.

The Village, on the banks of the Devon, is a
surprisingly hidden cluster of cottages, most dating
from the 19th century — with pantile roofs, skews and
random rubble walls — or from W. H. Henry's 1950s
reconstruction programme. The eastmost house is
grander, with a 1743 marriage stone.

Lornshill Farmhouse, c. 1770
A striking classical farmhouse on the south side of the
Tullibody to Alloa road, plain beneath steep, hipped
roof, save for its bay windows and Venetian doorway
(round headed flanked by narrow rectangular
windows).

King O'Muirs Farmhouse, near Glenochil, late
18th century
Plain two-storey harled farmhouse with hipped slate
roof and bowed centre window.

King O'Muirs Farmhouse.

The Blair.

THE HILLFOOTS

Sheltered in the lee of the Ochil Hills lie the Hillfoots villages of Blairlogie, Menstrie, Alva, Tillicoultry and Dollar. Each village grew around a fast-flowing burn, necessary for water and power for the meal mills and later woollen mills. The villages of Alva and Tillicoultry developed as small industrial textile towns. Each village usually enjoyed the patronage of a laird on whose ground it was built and who resided nearby. The old road from Stirling to Kinross passed through each village some way up the slope, and sections of it are still in use. In each village, the oldest cottages can be found at this level, some way uphill of the 1806 turnpike road.

Blairlogie

Just to the west of the District boundary, this tiny village is the first of the Hillfoots settlements, sheltering beneath Dumyat where the Ochils are at their most precipitous (see also *Stirling and Trossachs*).

72 The Blair, Alexander Spittal, 1546

A small tower house with a 1582 east wing. The original tower has an unusual stair-turret corbelled out at the south-east corner, the main roof and crowstepped gable continuing over and around. The initials A S and E H on the dormer windows are those of Alexander Spittal and his wife Elizabeth Hay, in whose family it remained until 1767. Legend accords the castle a secret chamber.

Since early this century, each Hillfoots burgh has been ascribed a distinguishing name: Alva — *The Model Burgh* after its *model lodging house;* Tillicoultry — *The Fountain Burgh* after its numerous fountains; and also *The Floral Burgh* in tribute to its displays of roses that line the main streets: and Dollar — *The Classic Burgh* after its Academy.

Glenochil, Cambus and Carsebridge Distilleries were three of the six lowland grain distilleries which amalgamated in 1877 to form Distillers Company Limited.

BLAIRLOGIE

Top: Watergate Cottage.
Right: Hillside and Crowsteps.
Above: Montana Cottage.

Below: Trade panel, Nethergate.
Right: Blairlogie Secession
Church.

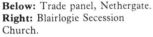

The Village, c. 1750-1900, forms a picturesque group of cottages in the lee of the castle, and promoted itself as a health resort. The villagers maintained a herd of about 50 goats, whose milk was tubercle free and ideal for consumptives, and rented out accommodation to visitors. The brisk mountain air was considered a bonus. The old High Road from Stirling to Kinross debouches into Blairlogie at a picturesque square, closed at the top by **Montana Cottage** misleadingly dated 1765. Its overhanging pantile roof, fine Italianate pilastered doorpiece and unusual oriel window represent a 20th century composition on earlier foundations. The date stone to one side of the window, has the initials J A and I T: on the other side is a sundial.

To the east of the square are a number of 18th century cottages, restored by Duncan Stirling: **Hillside,** 1976, is a conversion of two derelict cottages; **Crowsteps,** 1975, has an outside stair, slate roof, crowsteps and a sundial set into the wall: combined with the adjoining pair of low pantiled cottages it forms the **Village Hall. Fenham** is a recent adaptation of quaint old Boghead. **Blairlogie Cottage** to the west is a whitewashed 18th century house with hipped slate roof and classical doorpiece. **Watergate Cottage,** adjoining, is a 1979 hexagonal *Granny Flat* by Duncan Stirling. The old *Watergate* to the now overgrown well, has been preserved as a feature.

Blairlogie Secession Church, 1846
Plain with three pairs of double Gothic windows and
a bellcote adjoining the grander 1865 **Manse. Kirklea
Cottage,** 1758, is formed from a row of thatched and
pantiled tiny cottages. **Struan** has a row of eccentric
Gothic windows painted on its elongated dormer
window. **Nethergate,** formerly the Post Office, is
harled with sandstone architraves. A panel, built into a
small south wing, bearing the trade emblems of a
carpenter, dated 1728, and initialled I T and H B, was
removed from a cottage demolished when the nearby
classical **Telford House** was built, its name recalling
John Telford, a Stirling banker.

Powis House, 1746-47
A tall Scots mansion, with ashlar quoins and window
dressings, and Adam style interiors on the site of
Powhouse, the home of the Stirlings of Herbertshire.
The stable block, with its octagonal-roofed doocot, has
been converted into housing by Duncan Stirling.

Swan

Blairlogie Park, a classical villa in dressed stone, a
service wing behind, is set where the hillside is at its
steepest. A nearby cottage was demolished many years
ago by a rockfall, the boulder preserved in the picnic
area.

73 **Blairlogie House Hotel,** a rambling Gothicised
Victorian country house, developed out of the 18th
century Montague Cottage. The house passed through
many families, remembered in the hotel bedroom
names. Colonel Ian Hare and his wife Alice are
celebrated by a monogrammed fireplace in the bar and
the Colonel's ghost is said to *so enjoy* the house, it is
reluctant to leave.

74 **Redcar,** 1880, built for Sheriff T. B. Johnstone, sits
high above the road amid mature rhododenrons.
Gothic in style, with half-hipped and pitched red-tile
roofs, decorated ridge and paired windows. It cost
about £2,000 to blast a platform for the house out of
the hillside, but the unsurpassed view presumably
made it worthwhile.

Dumyat
*I can scarcely conceive nobler
prospects that there are from that
mountain,* wrote Lord Cockburn in
1838. *It is one of the many places
which make us not at all afraid to
boast of Scotland, even in comparison
with Switzerland. Our solitude and
elevation derived an additional charm
from the distant view of the people
sweltering below at the Stirling races.*

Robert Anderson, a native of
Tullibody, ran away to sea, having
got a girl with child. He made his
fortune as a shipmaster, trading in
Spain, where he was joined by his
brother-in-law, Edward Mayne of
Cambus. Mayne's nephew Edward
inherited most of the wealth: which
subsequently built Powis House.

Blairlogie Park.

Manor
Only a slag heap and an attractive
row of miners' housing
commemorates Manor, an ancient
defensive post and landing on the
Forth. *Manor, or Kingsnow House,
had been a Roman station, some
vestiges of the trenches being lately
visible. It was part of the lordship of
Stirling and feued by the Callenders
about 1479.* Ralph Dundas,
grandfather of Ramsay of
Ochtertyre, who wrote the above,
was the last to live at Manor, his
successor abandoning the old
house, or castle, in 1729 to build *a
small snug house at Airthrey* in
1747. He soon sold it to the
Haldanes, patrons of Robert Adam
(see *Stirling Guide),* from *the want
of proper relish for a country life.*
Ironically, Robert Haldane resold
the estate about 1796 to Dundas'
nephew, Sir Robert Abercromby,
and Airthrey subsequently
succeeded Tullibody as the
Abercromby seat.

MENSTRIE

Fowler

Menstrie Castle.

Menstrie

Menstry was feued from the Argyll
family by the father of the first Earl
of Stirling. This nobleman had an
uncommon share of taste for his
time. He made a terrace walk from
Myreton to Playgreen, which
commanded a delightful prospect of
the Forth and the country around.
Ramsay MSS.

In 1800 the diarist John Ramsay
of Ochtertyre visited Menstrie,
where he had spent much time in
the summer of 1752-53 *in my*
cheerful morn of youth when Mr
Abercromby and his wife lived there
in great credit and felicity. He found
the staircase up to the drawing room
ruinous, and everything bore the
marks of desolation . . . the rooms
where hospitality and kindness once
abode were waste or full of lumber.

A small village with a double origin: partly based on
the castle and its estate on the rich Forth carseland;
and partly on woollen manufacture.

75 **Menstrie Castle,** late 16th century
A sturdy picturesque, three-storey L-plan castellated
house, probably the rump of a full quadrangle,
entered through a wide-arched pend. After centuries of
neglect and misuse as a tenement, it was saved from
demolition by a campaign led by the actor Moultrie
Kelsall; its steep roof, crowstepped gables, dormer
windows and pepperpot turrets now restored. It thus
represents a large wealthy manor house, rather than a
castle that could have withstood a determined enemy.
Now domesticated by its cloistral setting amidst
W. H. Henry's pleasant 1957-60 square of housing,
it would originally have formed an impressive sight

CDC Libraries

Menstrie from the slopes of
Dumyat.

amidst these Forth flatlands. It contains a commemoration room to the Baronets of Nova Scotia, administered by the National Trust for Scotland, in recognition of the Castle as the birthplace of Sir William Alexander, founder of Nova Scotia.

Main Street

The Main Street effectively splits Menstrie into old and new. To the south of the road lie the principal housing estates: those of the 1950s and 1960s to the west, those of the 1970s and 1980s to the east. The latter are associated with the nearby **Glenochil Yeast Factory.** The Gothic **Primary School**, by Francis Mackison, 1875, has been replaced by a splendid new **Menstrie Primary School,** Central Region Architects, 1978: a warren of little classrooms and workspaces leading off communal central areas. **The Holly Tree Hotel** was refaced in the 1950s in Thirties style — reconstituted stone with horizontal windows, the door becoming part of the surround of the horizontal window above, while a single-storey parapeted bay window curves around the south-west corner. **The Co-operative Society Grocery** is ornamented by an exquisite two-face, triangular clock dated 1897. The **Parish Church and Hall,** narrow, long Victorian Gothic rectangles, with steep pitched roofs, decorated at the ridge line, and with low buttressed side walls, were designed by James Collie in 1880.

Midtown, old people's housing by W. H. Henry, is a group of cottage-inspired homes overlooking the landscaped area around the burn. The end house has the coat-of-arms stone of the Holburne family, with the motto *Decus meum virtus,* inserted in the gable end. Opposite is **Menstrie House,** Central Region Architects, 1982, more old people's housing near the burn: large rendered wings with red-tile hipped roofs and sitting areas identified by red-stained corner conservatories, whose rugged views contrast with the neat landscaping.

The Alexanders of Menstrie had been granted Menstrie c. 1500. It was probably during the teenage years of **William Alexander,** the statesman born at Menstrie in 1567, that this great new house was built. In 1584 he was appointed travelling companion to the eight-year-old Earl of Argyll on the latter's travels on the Continent. He subsequently ingratiated himself with the young James VI by his poetry on which he prided himself in endless philosophical strophes *in the manner of the Ancients.* He moved to England with the King in 1603, became Tutor to Prince Henry and was knighted in 1609. In 1625 he became Lieutenant of Nova Scotia and the following year, principal Secretary for Scotland. He was reviled, suspected of debasing the Scots coinage, and despite his elevation to Viscount Stirling and creation of a splendid new town house in Stirling itself (see *Stirling and the Trossachs*), he died a bankrupt.

Holburne panel, Midtown.
Below: Midtown.

James Holburne, a General in the Scots army against Cromwell, acquired Menstrie from Alexander's creditors in 1649, and the family, who sold the estate to the Abercrombies in 1719, are remembered by their coat-of-arms panel at Midtown — the site of Windsor Castle, probably their dower house. The last member of the family, Miss Mary Anne Barbara Holburne (d. 1882), of Bath, left part of her estate to endow Menstrie Parish Church, and with the remainder founded the Holburne of Menstrie Museum in Bath.

E

Menstrie played a small but significant role in establishing the textile industry in the Hillfoots. In 1800 the three Archibald brothers from Tullibody built their first woollen mill on the site between Menstrie burn and Brook Street, one of whom, John, had (with his sons) introduced the first local steam powered machinery at Menstrie.

Below: Broomhall.
Bottom: Menstrie House.
Below right: U.P. Mission Hall.

76 Elmbank Mill, c. 1865

Long, rectangular, and rubble built (once part of a much larger complex demolished in the early 1970s). Its north facade is reminiscent of a small Georgian country house. The Elmbank complex was founded by George Drummond as a gas-powered woollen mill in 1864, the boom period of Menstrie's textile industry. Drummond was joined and then succeeded by James Johnstone (builder of Broomhall).

100-102 and **104-106 Main Street** are almost identical Gothic cottages with porches, bay windows and canted dormer windows, with wrought-iron finials. The **U.P. Mission Hall** was designed by Adam Frame in 1891, also Gothic, but of pleasing proportions; the porch has a moulded arch and stone cross finial.

Ochil Road, the former main street, retains a few 18th and 19th century cottages, and continues into **New Row.** The rest have been rebuilt in W. H. Henry's pretty, sympathetic post-war style, which strove to find an acceptably modern Scottish idiom. The **Auld Brig,** 1665, is a rubble-built, humped-back single arch with an enscribed panel on the south. The stone walls of the 1642 corn mill can yet be spotted, just above the Auld Brig.

77 Broomhall, 1874, John Forbes, succeeded by Francis Mackison

That this splendid mill-owner's mansion (built for James Johnstone of Elmbank Mill) now stands as a magnificent hillside ruin seems to symbolise the fact that the mills are now as much a part of history as the Castle. Latterly used as Clifford Park boys' boarding school, it was burnt in 1940 while the boys were camping on the lawn. The lodge, boundary walls and gate piers remain, and the stables were converted into a house in 1977. Currently under conversion into a hotel by Bracewell Stirling Partnership.

RCAHMS

ALVA

The centre of historic Alva, as with all the Hillfoot communities, is uphill from the main road (Stirling Street) where the old road (Back Road, Beauclerc Street, Ochil Road) crosses the Alva Burn at the entrance to the Glen. The Parish Church was along to the east on the edge of the community. It is clustered around the burn — Green Square, Erskine Street, Beauclerc Street, the Island and Brook Street — that one finds traces of old Alva. Its origins derive partly from the influence of the great lairds of Alva House, about half a mile to the east, and partly to the mills — the finest of which stands silhouetted against the hills, dominating the entire town: the Strude Mill.

Alva House (demolished)

A tower house, certainly extant in 1542, was incorporated into Sir Charles Erskine's new mansion of 1636, which in turn became the east wing of Alva House when the Johnstones added the huge south front and west wing c. 1820. Miss Carrie Johnstone inherited the house and estate in 1890 and although she is still fondly remembered for her kindness, she overspent so considerably that on her death in 1929, the sale of the estate and house contents did not pay her debts. The house could not be sold and eventually collapsed during the war when used for military target practice.

CDC Libraries

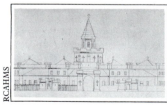

RCAHMS

Top: Alva House and Sauchie Tower drawn by Anthony Stuart 1790.
Centre: Alva House.
Above: Castellated stableblock as proposed for Alva House by R. & J. Adam, 1789.

Top: Alva House Stables.
Above: St Serf's Parish Church.
Right: Johnstone Mausoleum.

The first **Erskine of Alva,** Sir Charles, a younger son of the 2nd Earl of Mar, bought the estate in 1636 and became keeper of Cambuskenneth Abbey which had been granted to the 1st Earl at the Reformation (see *Stirling Guide*). Erskine's son, also Sir Charles, became a Baronet of Nova Scotia in 1666 and had four remarkable sons. The eldest, Sir James was killed at the Battle of Landen in 1693. **Sir John Erskine** (1672-1739), a Jacobite, is remembered for his discovery of an *exceedingly rich* vein of silver in the hills above Alva, from which he had extracted the value of about £4,000 per week, from 1710, to which he owed his pardon for his part in the 1715 Jacobite Uprising. *He was a man of more genius than conduct, of more wit than wisdom,* wrote John Ramsay of Ochtertyre, *but the heat and volatility of his fancy would not be regulated by prudential considerations.*

The house was situated in beautiful surroundings, high on the wooded hillside, embracing extensive views. Its pleasure grounds included long formal avenues, to east and west, fountains, terraces, flower gardens and rare trees. Plans were prepared by Robert and James Adam in 1789 to refront the House and build a castellated stable block, but the only built part of the project seems to have been the Johnstone Mausoleum.

79 **Alva House Stables,** c. 1820, probably by William Stirling
A symmetrical rectangular courtyard block with projecting towers to the centre and wings of the frontage. The ground floor provided stabling for seventeen horses as well as two coach houses, harness rooms and later, garage accommodation. On the first floor was housing for the coachman, butler, gamekeeper and grooms. The remains of a doocot can be seen above the arched central carriageway entrance. The stable block is to be renovated as a principal feature of the **Ochil Hills Woodland Park,** formed from the woodlands of Alva House Estate, which is provided with waymarked forest walks and visitor facilities. Within the Park there still stand the 18th century **Ice House,** and the brick walls of the 19th century kitchen garden. Leaflet available.

St Serf's Parish Church, rebuilt from 1631-32 (now demolished)
Plain Georgian, with Gothic ornamentation representing an 1815 rebuilding probably by William Stirling, which incorporated the 1632 sanctuary. Victorian additions included twin low square towers in the re-entrant angles. In 1981 the congregation merged with that of the Eadie Church in Alva, and St Serf's Church, badly affected by dry rot, was abandoned. It

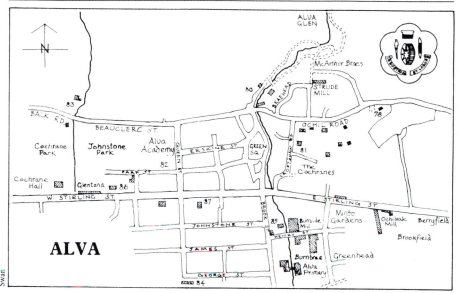

ALVA

was damaged by fire in 1985 and subsequently demolished.

78 Johnstone Mausoleum, Robert and James Adam, 1790
A small, square groin-vaulted building of two storeys, the memorials being on the upper. The entrance arch is framed by Doric columns supporting a triangular pediment; and in the north and south walls are empty pedimented niches. The Johnstone crests on the gates were originally on the gates to Alva House, removed to Johnstone Park when the house was demolished, but later resetted here.

Alva Glen is an attractive nature walk of tree-lined paths carved out of the steep rock faces and narrow bridges over steep gorges. At the entrance to Alva Glen is the Eadie Memorial Fountain.

80 Island House, mid-18th century, is reputed to have been the first house in Alva taller than a single storey, and thereby christened *The Castle*. Two storeys of local whinstone, and walls two foot thick, the house sat guarding the entrance to the Glen and provided four very crowded dwellings of one or two rooms each. Absorbed by Cunningham's Longbank Printworks in the 1930s, it now accommodates a film studio. The **Island** is a row of harled and slated cottages by the Alva Burn, the eastmost one was the smithy of Robert Porteous, grandfather of the builder of Meadow Mill.

Sir John Erskine's neighbour, probably Abercromby of Tullibody, remarked of his estate improvements: *Sir John, all this is very fine and practicable, but it would require a princely fortune,* to which the reply: *George, when I first formed my scheme of policy for this place, I was drawing such sums out of the mine that I could not help looking upon the Elector of Hanover as a small man.* His ambitious projects, which included a canal between the Devon and his coal mines, and extensive agricultural enclosures and improvements, absorbed most of his wealth. His son, Sir Henry, the 5th baronet, was a fashionable figure in London political circles, said by Horace Walpole to be *a military poet and a creature of Lord Bute's.* The Alva baronetcy ended with Sir John's grandson, Sir James Erskine, who succeeded his maternal uncle as 2nd Earl of Rosslyn in 1805.

ALVA

The Woollen Industry in Alva

By the 1790s, the Hillfoots villages used the combination of hills for sheep grazing, steep burns for water power and the proximity of a huge market in the Central Belt, to create a very early concentration of industrial revolution activity. It became a major woollen manufacturing district. Alva had the most weavers (67 as compared with Tillicoultry's 21) producing handwoven cloth, or serge, and blankets from cottage-based looms. The first Alva woollen mills were built c. 1800, and from 1815 water was used to power the spinning machinery. By 1830 Alva had nine water-powered spinning mills, although the vast bulk of the wool was by now imported.

In the 1820s the local landowner, James Johnstone, keen to help develop the industry, opened up Alva Glen as a source of waterpower by blasting away rock faces and constructing a dam from which water was conveyed to the mills along wooden troughs or lades. The water power was gradually supplemented by, then superseded by, coal-fired steam power in the latter half of the 19th century. The woollen mills then developed in other areas of the town, notable examples being the Glentana Works and the brick-built mills around Henry Street.

Right: Strude Mill.

Of Sir John's brothers **Robert Erskine** (1677-1718) was physician to Peter the Great of Russia, and Charles Erskine (1680-1763), **Lord Tinwald,** afterwards Lord Justice Clerk, bought the Alva Estate about 1749 from his nephew. Ramsay noted that he was *one of the most distinguished characters of those times,* but that *A fastidious critic might think there was sometimes too much art and 'finesse' in his way of expressing himself.* Lord Tinwald's son James was also Lord Justice Clerk, taking the name **Lord Barjarg,** and later Lord Alva, the last Erskine of Alva.

Fowler

Strude (or Boll) Mill, c. 1820

The glory of Alva: outside places like New Lanark, Scottish mills rarely rose to the classical dignity of this six-storey, 25 window long mill, built in squared rubble with dressed stone. Its commanding presence is emphasised by the central four bays being capped by a pediment and bellcote. It was only part of a larger group of mill buildings owned by William Archibald & Son until 1976. At each window there was a handloom but the tradition that there were 365 windows, one for each day of the year, is over optimistic.

East of the Burn

The cottages along **Ochil Road** are 19th century remnants of Alva's first ribbon development. The houses along the south side are mill owners' 19th century mansions with large gardens and outbuildings. The **Manse** is 1950s on the old site, while **Glenside and Balnagowan** are late Victorian Gothic mansions. **Craigknowe,** 1939-40, one of William Kerr's last commissions, is a white harled brick cottage with little dormers in its rambling slate roof, a bay window to the sitting room. It is quite isolated within a steep terraced garden overlooking the Devon Valley, at the end of a long tree-lined drive squeezed from a neighbouring garden. The Gothic **Ochilbank,** 1820, was built for the Johnstone family as a home for a younger son (James Raymond Johnstone having 16 children), extended about 1860. **Kenmuir,** 1813, and **Bernard Cottage** are two-storey, white-harled Georgian.

Croftshaw Road

Off the track leading back down to the main road are [81] two grand late-Victorian mansion houses. **Edgehill,** c. 1870, is Gothicised with parapeted bay windows, decorated ridge line and wrought-iron ornamentation over the door. **Lynwood,** at the end of L'Estrange Terrace, is of a similar age and style, no less grand, but more secluded.

The Cochranes, James Shearer, 1947-50

A pretty series of cottages and taller blocks built as retirement homes by the Cochrane Foundation, in well-detailed stonework with pantiled hipped roofs.

Robertson Street is a row of 1870s weavers' cottages, running north to the Strude Mill.
Braehead, Burgh Architect, 1938, are flat-roofed terraces of stepped two-storey houses, ascending the hillside. Each terrace is alternately painted in ochre and umber.

Upper Brook Street, formerly Boll Lane, was the centre for the water-powered woollen mills, and many old foundations can still be seen. The brick-built engineering works at the head of Brook Street were grafted onto the 1829 Alva Village jail.

Braehead.

The Cochrane Foundation
administers the 1942 bequest of three brothers Cochrane — James, Charles and John — whose parents emigrated to Albany, New York State in the 1860s. The family prospered, originally through manufacturing shawls, an art presumably learnt in Alva. The brothers, latterly of Philadelphia, made numerous gifts to Alva, especially the Cochrane Park and Hall. John Cochrane was named after his uncle, Dr John Eadie.

The Boll Bell Inscription
The Boll, or Strude Mill bell is preserved at the Cochranes, with a Lallans inscription (1963) by Alva poet James Nicol Jarvie:

*For a hunner year an mair it was
    this
bell that waukened the Douce A'va
    folk
Airly Ilka Mornin, binna the
    Sabbath,
Til Anither Darg and lowsd' Them
    Ilka nicht.
Aa that time the Bell hung heigh on
the Boll Mill Bot or it micht faa.
It wis brocht doon an stans here
Amang folk that anes Kenn'd it weel:
Its auld tongue, Quate Noo is Bot a
Ghaist-soond i' mony an A'va
    Memory.*

Edgehill.

The Johnstones of Alva

Aged 16, **John Johnstone** (1734-1795), 5th son of a Lanarkshire laird, went to Calcutta as an artillery officer, and in 1757, *aided much to the success of the battle of Plassey,* under Robert Clive, although he later joined the *storm of obloquey* against Clive in the 1770s. He prudently waited until after Clive's suicide in 1774 before spending the vast fortune he *earnt* in India. In 1778 he added Alva to his Selkirk and Dumfriesshire estates, and yet in 1788 still remained *immensely rich* with a fortune of £300,000. His son, **James Raymond Johnstone** (1768-1830) had 16 children, of which the eldest, James (1801-1888), took Sarah Mary L'Estrange as his second wife in 1862 against strong competition in Brussels from a *foreign royal prince!*

Top: The Old Town c. 1920.
Below: Swimming Pool.
Bottom: Barnaigh.

Robertson

Fowler

Swan

Some former handloom weaving sheds and weavers' cottages survive in **Erskine Street. No. 5 Inn,** c. 1900, modernised beyond recognition, commemorates Robert Burns' visit to Alva in 1787. Dominating the end of Erskine Street, but really bounded by Queen Street and Park Street, is the 1969 **Alva Academy,** designed by the County Architect: one, two and three-storey, flat roofed blocks typical of that period are brought to a climax by the monstrous concrete frame of the water tower. The entrance court is presided over by the 1980 **Swimming Pool** and **Leisure Centre,** by the Regional Architect. The bold concrete buttressing frames a building remarkable for its utilisation of solar energy in this northern climate,

Beauclerc Street was feued by James Johnstone from 1796. Originally Back Raw, it was renamed after Johnstone's daughter, Lady Jemima Beauclerc. Running westwards from the burn, the Street is formed of groups of little cottages, some with dormer windows and porches. **Barnaigh,** an 1860s mansion barely visible through the tall trees and shrubs of its large terraced garden at the foot of the Carnaughton Glen, is a splendid example of high Victorian eclecticism: a grand Italianate tower to the south-east with mock canon gargoyles sparring with its tall, piended French chateau roof. The rainwater heads are bearded with angelic wings above spirated downpipes. **Listerlea,** 1873, a substantial Gothicised villa, now within Cochrane Park, was built as a Manse.

As the **Back Road,** the old road continues westwards, now hosting a series of individual modern villas and chalets, each identified by an ostentatious name. The resounding **Jinglebank** is timber and stone clad, while **Balbaird** is a dark brick pavilion.

Expansion to the South

The arrival of the new Hillfoots main road in 1806 pulled Alva south from Green Square to the new Stirling Street. The lairds were quick to seize the opportunity of raising capital and James Johnstone offered the first feus in the same year. The resulting buildings were usually simple, undecorated Scots Georgian houses, unified by an almost identical Doric pilastered doorway which occurs, less frequently, in similar aged houses throughout Alva and Tillicoultry. Streets of millworkers' cottages named after the Johnstone family were laid out during the late 19th century to the south of the main road. Most were redeveloped for housing by the local authorities during the 1960s and 70s. The old **Railway Station** in George Street, which ended the 1863 line from Alloa by Cambus, has been converted into a garage. The Alva railway branch was prevented from joining the east-going line at Tillicoultry by James Johnstone who forbade it pass through his Alva Estate.

Brook Street, the direct road into Alva from Alloa, the entry marked by **The Boll,** a neat Gothicised farmhouse (c. 1850), now part of the outskirts of the town. Behind is an attractive enclosed steading of rough white-washed buildings used for stabling, and a farm shop.

Green Square and Alva Green

About 1700 the then Laird of Alva, Sir John Erskine, decided to lay out a village in the form of a square; that became Green Square (although only the north and west sides were built at first), located immediately behind the present Johnstone Arms Hotel. The area around Alva Green was feued for housing by weavers (predominantly), labourers and craftsmen, during the 18th century and the pattern was continued by the new Johnstone lairds of the 19th century. In 1770-76, the Erskines feued out the south side of the old road, their plan being to extend the village north of Green Square by granting simple feus to anyone prepared to build. Duke Street (or Middle Row) had only to be sufficiently wide *sae that a horse and a sack of meal on his back could pass,* and the feu duty could be paid in *kain hens good and sufficient, or fit for the spit when delivered.* It was claimed to be the narrowest named street in Scotland.

Fowler

Alva Primary School, Central Region Architects, 1976

Alva Primary School.

A friendly complex of a one-storey hall and classroom courtyard block, with an enclosed bridge over the Alva Burn leading to a two-storey block of more senior classrooms, designed in crisp rectangular blocks of dark brickwork, on the site of the Meadow Mill. A link with the past is formed by the retention of the ancient school bell as a feature within the entrance foyer.

ALVA

Burnside Works.

Right: Greenfield Mill.

In **Henry Street,** a number of 19th century textile mills were built in the locality of the burn. The red and white brick **Burnbrae Works,** 1867 and 1920, was originally built for handloom weaving. Warp knitting machines were soon introduced, driven by overhead shafts, which still power the modern electric knitting machines of Dolf Textiles. **Burnside Works,** on the north side is a very similar contemporary brick 85 woollen mill, threatened with demolition. **Greenfield Mill,** also disused, is an eight-window, rubble block dating from the early 19th century. At the northern corner with Brook Street is an 1830 stone handloom weaving mill, a later dwellinghouse at one end.

Stirling Street
Cochrane Hall, West Stirling Street, William Kerr, 1929

A cross between South African and Home Counties vernacular, completely out of character with the Hillfoots whose verticality is acknowledged in its dramatic steep roof. That roof is the dominant feature: hipped to the sides rising into half gables, extending over little hipped wings to the front at either side, and rising over a huge curved, gabled projecting porch. Wooden columns form a verandah between the porch and the wings. The **Public Conveniences** by the District Architect, 1984, is a neat little block with a circular window, the green-stained timber front office doubling as the Putting Green Attendant's desk.

86 **Glentana Mills,** West Stirling Street, 1874
A fifteen window powerloom shed fronts the main road, well detailed in two-tone brick, with an attractive corbelled cornice and recessed windows. It may have been designed by Glasgow architect Robert Baldie in 1887, with the old smithy and the engine house behind.

121 Stirling Street, adjoining the Eadie Church.

Dr John Eadie (1810-76), distinguished theological professor in Glasgow, was the son of an Alva road-mender. Well known in the United Presbyterian church, Eadie became a supporter of Biblical Criticism and a contributor to the publication in 1881 of the Revised Version of the English Bible.

87 **The Eadie Church,** 1842, replaced St Serf's as the
Parish Church following the amalgamation of the
congregations. It looks suitably forbidding with its
mixture of Gothic pinnacles, arches and castellations.
The adjoining house is of the original new road
feuing. The Alva Co-operative Bazaar Society was
founded in 1845, and grew in strength, represented by
the present buildings, dominating Stirling Street,
which date from 1888 and 1895. **Alva Glen Hotel,**
1807, was built as the Blue Bell Tavern to serve the
first travellers on the new road, its finely sculpted
ornamentation at cornice level and around the door
lost under paintwork.

Greenhead.

Minto Gardens, 1919, is a pioneering example of
Addison Act houses designed by William Kerr for
Alva Burgh Council: conventional, solid, two-storey
blocks. Nearby **Greenhead** is something different —
solid two-storey blocks, but with the flat roofs,
exposed brickwork and wide sweeping bands of
harling above regular horizontal windows of the
Thirties.

The **Eastern Approach** contains a number of textile
mills, old and new. **Interbobbin,** 1985, in Alva's new
industrial park, is a cuboid of brick and rust-coloured
cladding, much enhanced by the S.D.A. landscaping.
Berryfield is the 1974 Coblecrook Dyeworks,
dominated by a tall square chimney. Part of the yard
at **Brookfield** contains relics of Ross' 1865 spinning
mills. Hodgson's (formerly Archibald's) **Ochilvale
Mills,** was built at the end of the 19th century, the
main block being of red and white brick; the **Mill
Shop** is created from the rubble-built wool store.

Cochrane Hall.

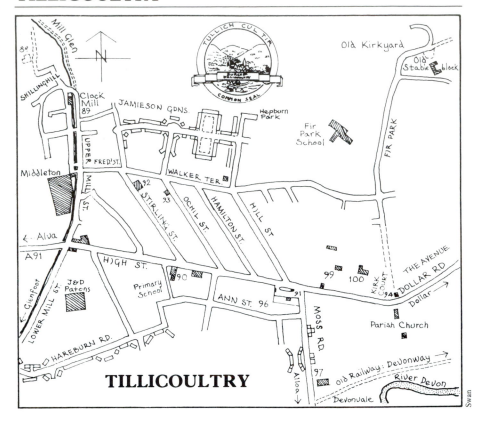

TILLICOULTRY

Survey drawings of motte-and-bailey castle excavated at Castle Craig.

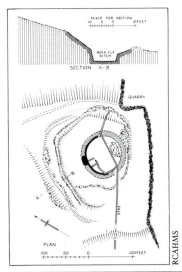

Like other Hillfoot communities, modern Tillicoultry owes its existence to the fast-running burns tumbling down the Ochils to join the River Devon in the valley. To appreciate its real character, visitors have to leave the wide main road and penetrate uphill. It developed from the small village of Westerton at the upper part of Tillicoultry Burn, by the Middleton and Clock Mills, where the old Stirling High Road passed over Middleton Bridge and cut along what is now Frederick Street. An ancient fortress is known to have existed on Castle Craig above, perpetuated in the names of the early 19th century textile mills. The parish was formed by three villages: Westerton, Coalsnaughton on the ridge to the south; and Easterton, which no longer exists, but near Harviestoun.

Eight woollen mills were established by the Tillicoultry Burn of which the only ones to survive are the **Clock Mill** (1824) and **Middleton Mill** (from 1836) in Upper Mill Street; **J. & D. Paton's Mill** (from 1825) and the **Oak Mill** (from 1873) in Lower Mill Street. Paton's Mill alone still produces knitwear, although elsewhere other firms manufacture textiles

from buildings adapted for the purpose. The
88 foundations of **Craigfoot Mill** (1808 and 1838) can
still be seen just below Tillicoultry Quarry, which has
been gouging aggregate and dressed stone from the
Ochils since 1880. This and other mills were powered
by water brought along a timber lade and aqueduct
from the 1824 dam in Mill Glen. The massive iron
water wheel at Craigfoot was 30 ft in diameter.

The Mill Glen, Arthur Bracewell, 1926
Spectacular walk of bridges, paths and steps
engineered by Bracewell, provide a route amid rare
plants and wildlife into the rolling Ochils. The first
bridge is a fine stone arch with a plaque
commemorating the Glen opening. A nature trail
within the Glen has been created, where the remains
of the timber dam can be seen. Guide booklet
available.

Upper Mill Street
The Clock Mill, 1824
Built by James and George Walker from Galashiels to
manufacture blankets, plaids and tartan shawls, its
gable, with clock and ball finial, faces downhill. The
Mill was powered both from the mill lade and by an
engine house (now gone) driven by a series of
underground shafts. Now the centre of the Hillfoots
Mill Heritage Trail, it houses a Tourist Information
Centre, a District Council exhibition of the history of
the textile industry, and craft workshops for textile
related small businesses (opened 1986). Leaflet to Mill
Heritage Trail available.

Swan

Above: Remains of the dam, Mill
Glen.
Left: Shillinghill.
Below: Clock Mill.

Swan

Middleton Mills, 1836
A complex of rubble buildings built by Robert
Archibald and Sons who moved from the 1805
Middleton Mill, which was later incorporated. From
1934 it was used by a Samuel Jones subsidiary — the
Dunedin Stationery Company. The entrance offices
were designed by Arthur Bracewell in 1926.

Shillinghill, off Upper Mill Street, has attractive
stone faced, white rendered houses designed by A. G.
Bracewell, 1957-58, for the Burgh Council in a

Fowler

77

Cairnton Place, refurbished by Bracewell Stirling Partnership, 1975.

conscious attempt to retain some of the historic flavour of the Old Town. The nearby gardens by the burn, 1970, were formed from a bequest from Tillicoultry's longest serving Town Councillor, William Jamieson. A variety of old cottages, mostly early 19th century, can be found in Glassford Square, Cairnton Place, Frederick Street and Crofthead. The 89 **Woolpack,** an old weavers' inn, is a charming little two-storey hostelry within the clustered cottages of **Glassford Square,** redolent of the days when wool was brought across the Ochils from Blackford by pack horse.

J. & D. Paton's Mill, Lower Mill Street, 1836
This enormously long, 34 window, low rubble mill is part of what was once the most productive textile mill in Scotland, that of James and David Paton of Alloa. The Gold Medal which Patons won in the Great Exhibition in 1851 symbolised the international reputation of their shawls, tartans and tweeds. In the 20th century Patons produced tartans and serges, notably for military use during the First World War. Now a knitwear mill and millshop.

High Street
The principal businesses emigrated south to the new highway after it was built in 1806. Tillicoultry enjoyed few grand houses, as there were only a handful of mill owning families, and textile mills were Tillicoultry's only industry until the 1920s. Consequently, the majority of buildings in the High Street were purely utilitarian commercial premises, with little notion of architectural quality. Many were replaced in the late 1960s by widely spaced three-storey blocks of housing.

Below: High Street.
Bottom: Former West Church.

Tillicoultry's hotels are all clustered together to serve custom on the new road: the **Royal Arms** and the **Crown Hotel** are on the north side of High Street, and the **Castle Craig Hotel** is opposite. All are two-storey, with plain margins and Doric doors. The **Tillicoultry Co-operative Society** (the first co-operative in Clackmannanshire and one of the first in Scotland) inhabits two plain blocks, one dated 1838.

District Library, High Street, c. 1830, is formed from a group of three imposing Georgian houses, pink harled, with painted margins and quoins. The eastmost part has a fluted Doric-columned porch, and some of the windows have been altered. The elegant, 90 classically rectangular, 1840 **West Church** was converted in 1982 by Alex Strang Associates into sheltered housing for the elderly. The upper parts of the windows have been graced with reflective glass to conceal the lowered ceilings within.

CDC Libraries

Murray Square, 1952.

91 Murray Square, from 1930
One of the first bus stations in Scotland, instigated by
Provost Thomas Murray who was worried at the
danger of accidents occurring from the eight bus
services (334 buses daily) which used Tillicoultry as a
terminus at that time. Murray gifted the prefabricated
Clock, 1931, **Rose and Rock Gardens,** and **The
Thomas Murray Howff for Aged Men,** 1936, a
little octagonal reading room. Excepting the clock, the
buildings were all designed by Arthur Bracewell, the
most interesting being the sadly vandalised **Bus
Shelter.**

The Village Expansion — Weavers' Cottages
From the 1840s a wealthier class of mill worker
appeared in Tillicoultry, able to afford to buy or rent
a small cottage, and new streets were built at an
oblique angle to the north of High Street.

Stirling Street has single and double cottages to the
west with canted attic dormers. The east (or sunny)
side has grander houses and cottages. The former
92 Walker Institute, c. 1850, is a Gothicised house,
extended in 1919 by William Kerr in neat Renaissance
style. The old **Free Church,** 1844, identified by
its unusual iron-columned hexagonal belfry, lost its
congregation to the West Church in 1909 and since
then has been part of a knitwear factory. Ironic that
this symbol of stoic puritanism should now have been
acquired by Laura Ashley, whose self-indulgent mill-
maids would have anathematised the Seceders.

The Tillicoultry Flood
In August 1877 *one of the most
calamitous floods took place along the
front of the Ochil range that was
ever known to man . . . after a
deluging rain had continued for some
time . . . Tillicoultry Burn came
raging down in one almighty wall of
water of some seven or eight feet
high, carrying everything before
it. . . .* The flood swept away large
sections of Upper Mill Street;
houses, bridges and the Castle
Mill, and tragically drowning the
mill owner and a mill hand.

Walker Institute extension.

Swan

Fowler

Ben Cleuch, the highest Ochil Peak (2,363 ft), was to have a railway to its summit. The line was surveyed in 1863 in the hope that *the scheme will be carried through, as it will bring our beautiful Ochils more into notice . . . and attract crowd of tourists to our really picturesque neighbourhood.* Fortunately for the *beautiful Ochils* this was one engineering proposition the Victorians abandoned.

Swan

Top: Tower, Ochil Street.
Above: 1920 housing block, Hill Street.

93 **Tower,** Ochil Street, John Melvin, 1879.
A competition-winning Victorian curiosity, donated by mill owner James Archibald as a campanile to the 1859 Town Hall (demolished 1986). Square at the lower stages, rising to a balcony decorated by four tiny turrets, the tower continues as a louvred octagon to a four-faced clock and parapet, recently restored.
Ochil Street, mid 19th century, is perhaps the finest of the Tillicoultry planned weavers' streets: stone cottages with regular slate roofs, each with a neat front garden. The plainer, later cottages of **Hamilton Street,** forgo their front gardens.

Hill Street, late 19th century, is a mixture of cottages and houses some with front gardens, some not, and some with minor ornament. Two of the first housing blocks in Tillicoultry designed by William Kerr following the 1919 Addison Act on the east side.

Walker Terrace, late 19th century
A row of larger Victorian villas with Gothic elements built along the old Hillfoots high road. No. 38 (originally a manse but now the offices of Bracewell Stirling Partnership) is a fine Gothic villa, with decorated ridge, front gable and bay window, designed by Adam Frame in 1889.

Jamieson Gardens, Arthur Bracewell, 1931-39
Unremarkable individually, although the decorative door mouldings are a particular delight, the real value

of this five-phase housing development is its Garden City layout. **Scheme No. 1,** 1931, consists of seven blocks at the half crescented junction of Cairnton Place. **Scheme No. 2,** 1932, continues eastwards, two blocks of houses on each side of the road, with pedimented gables above the entrances. **Scheme No. 3,** 1933, forms a crescent opposite Ochilview Road and is distinguished by projecting door lintels. **Scheme No. 5,** 1939, superseding an unbuilt scheme, completed the Arthur Bracewell part of Jamieson Gardens and Ochilview Road. The east-west road continued through a dramatic rectangle. To north and south are wide grassed areas with long terraces of brick housing. The last three blocks were a 1941 amendment, war shortages compelling concrete beam floors, flat roofs and concrete stairs in place of the pitched roofs and floors of timber construction.

1723 headstone in the Old Kirkyard, with the ploughshare, colter and harrow of the ploughman.
Below: Scheme No. 2, Jamieson Gardens.

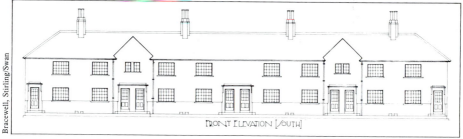

FRONT ELEVATION [/OUTH]

Fir Park School, W. H. Henry, County Architect, 1966

A composition of rectangular, single-storey brick boxes enfolding a four-storey one, now an annexe to Alva Academy. Alva Academy provides secondary education for all Hillfoots towns, Fir Park presently accommodating the first year. The dry ski slope, 1985, provides a useful (if unsightly) facility. The **Fir Park Estate,** A. G. Bracewell, 1967-68, is private housing meandering up the steep hillside towards the old kirkyard; simple bungalows to the east: Alpine, flat roofed chalets to the west, stepped down on account of the gradient.

The Old Kirkyard, Mediaeval onwards

Well worth the climb up the steep hill. Site of the Parish Church from the 11th century to 1773, the Kirkyard contains some interesting stones, including a 12th century hog-backed stone with a ridge down the centre, and a 1522 baker's stone.

Tillicoultry House, 1829 (demolished)

A very plain, classical house de-roofed then demolished after the last laird quit the district in 1938. All that now remains is the tall retaining wall of the garden and the fine classical **Stableblock**

Tillicoultry was an early centre of Hillfoots textiles, its first mill established in the 1790s. Between 1801 and 1851 the population of Tillicoultry increased from 916 to 4,686, an expansion responsible for much of the current architectural character of the town. It remained an important manufacturing centre after being overtaken in importance by Alva in mid-century. The first mills were built next to the burn for water power, but were superseded by steam powered mills in the 1830s. As the upper environs of the burns were already occupied, new sites were found lower down the burn and to the south-east of the town. Devonside was established as a village to accommodate the new influx on the south bank of the Devon, steam powered mills being in operation there by the 1830s. The high peak of textile manufacturing was reached around 1900, since when it has declined, here, to virtual extinction.

CDC Tech Services

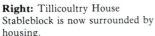

RCAHMS

(converted into flats). The west front is arched, flanked by blank archways and topped with a splendid cupola. The horses had the better bargain. The 94 **Lodge,** early 19th century, possibly by William Stirling, has an overscaled pedimented doorway facing the Parish Church.

Right: Tillicoultry House Stableblock is now surrounded by housing.
Above: Detail of cupola.
Below: Devonvale Hall.

95 **Tillicoultry Mains,** William Stirling, 1837-88
A delightful Georgian three-sided steading, the east and west ranges being of one-storey ending in higher pavilions. The north range has arched cartsheds with grain lofts above.

Devonvale Mill and Moss Road

I think that for beauty, our southern style of building with its plentiful supply of windows, white enamelling, rustic arches and red roofs, takes a lot of beating, though naturally Scots houses are of necessity built for strength and warmth. Thus Sidney Platfoot (d. 1963), two years after moving to Tillicoultry from Camberwell in 1923, as the Managing Director of a new paper coating firm — Samuel Jones and Co. (Devonvale) Ltd. Recognising the value of a contented workforce, Platfoot set about establishing facilities for its benefit. He employed the talents of a Lethaby-trained architect, **Arthur Bracewell** (1891-1953), who had been brought north to Tillicoultry in 1925 by the Salts of Saltaire, then owners of Middleton and Devonpark Mills, to renovate and design minor extensions. Platfoot's repeated motto, in product and building alike, was *Devonvale means quality.*

South of the Main Road

96 **Collier's Court,** District Council Architects, 1984, provides an excellent courtyard of self-professed Pittenweem vernacular, surrounding a harbour of children's play equipment. **Stoneyacre,** Arthur Bracewell, 1932-34, has Garden City housing blocks, similar to Jamieson Gardens. The **Hareburn Road** houses nearest Lower Mill Street are excellent examples of formal blocks, with great central entrances approached by long pathways.

Fowler

Moss Road, Arthur Bracewell, from 1934
Designed to the requirements of Sidney Platfoot of
Devonvale, these houses display a fine sense of social
status in their variety — some management and some
workers. **36-46 Moss Road,** 1935, are three double
villas with parapeted curved bay windows to each
side. **52-62 Moss Road,** 1937, comprise two unique
triple villas, with distinguishing 1930s curved bays.
Bracewell designed **Devonvale Crescent,** in 1939,
built 1946-53, as two back-to-back crescents of houses
forming a built realisation of the butterfly, the Samuel
Jones symbol. **The Recreation Ground** was acquired
by Platfoot in 1925 to safeguard future expansion,
using it in the meantime for football, cricket pitches, a
bowling green and tennis courts — each with its
elegant pavilion. The bowling facilities alone survive.
The 1964 **West Mill** is the expected expansion,
designed by Arthur Bracewell's son, A. G. Bracewell.
Devonvale War Memorial, by C. d'O Pilkington
Jackson, is Platfoot's tribute to those of his workers
who fell during the Second World War, forming the
97 entrance gates to the Recreation Grounds. **Devonvale
Hall,** Arthur Bracewell, 1940, displays the company's
Camberwell Beauty butterfly above and traces of
modernism around the entrance.

Top: Collier's Court.
Above: The 1948 tennis pavilion
is survived by its sister bowling
pavilion.
Left: Devonvale Mills, c. 1880.
Below: The Butterfly Inn.

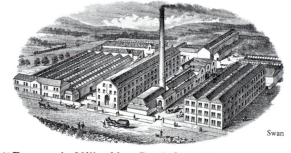

Swan

98 **Devonvale Mills,** Moss Road, from 1846
A large three-storey, six by sixteen window, white-
painted stone building, with associated buildings of
the 1860s. Established by J. & R. Archibald,
Devonvale Mill concentrated on tweed manufacture
for which it became famous. It was used as an army
barracks during the First World War, the ground floor
providing stabling for 800 horses, and in 1920 Samuel
Jones of Camberwell purchased it for a papercoating
plant. The mill buildings provide sound, sterling use
as a thriving furniture retail company, whose
advertising campaigns have brought Tillicoultry an
influx of visitors. The **Butterfly Inn,** A. G.
Bracewell, 1954, is converted from the works canteen
and traps a ceramic butterfly on its gable.

Swan

Top: Kirk Court, with Beechwood behind.
Above: St Serf's Parish Church.

Dollar Road
99 **Westbourne,** probably by John Melvin, 1868
A small but grand Gothic Scots house with castellated bay windows, whose gate lodge gives an over-opulent effect. The stables were converted by A. G. Bracewell 100 to his own house. **Beechwood,** 1860-70, by Adam Frame, is the largest house in Tillicoultry, originally an asymmetrical Gothic building with square bay to the west. The large extension to the west and north doubled the house in size. Some exceptional plasterwork inside. **Kirk Court** by Duncan Stirling, 1985, is a three-sided courtyard of staggered, terraced brick sheltered houses, **The Avenue,** Duncan Stirling, 1984, continues the Kirk Court aesthetic, one-person houses using the miners' row idiom, and the hill to stagger the roof line: formal entrances, pathways and gardens to the north and a large sunny private drying green to the south.

St Serf's Parish Church, Dollar Road, William Stirling, 1827-29
Replacing the 1773 church in neo-perpendicular Gothic, the impressive features of the church are the large octagonal bellcote to the north end and the buttressing to the sides of each bay which continue into pointed finials, high above the building. The **Manse** dates from 1811.

Dollar Road Bungalows, Arthur Bracewell, 1933-51
Nine private bungalows built by Devonvale Contractors (a subsidiary of Samuel Jones), the last one **Broomhall** (No. 44), 1940, built for Horace Platfoot, director and son of the Devonvale Mill Managing Director. The plan is in the form of a butterfly.

Devonside, from 1834
A small village on the southern bank of the River Devon formed when the first carding and spinning mill was established downhill from Tillicoultry. Within two years, five factories were carding, spinning, weaving and dyeing on the site; with the Devonvale Mill across the Devon. Some were later amalgamated into **Devonpark Mill.**

Coalsnaughton
The third village of Tillicoultry Parish, high on the south ridge above the valley, is reached by a steep and winding road from Devonside. Its name derived from *Collie Nechtan* — the wood of Nechtan — possibly after the famous Pictish King Nechtan Macderile. Until the 1950s, the village core consisted of small cottages, many whitewashed and pantiled (one had RDED 1683 over its lintel), and 19th century miners'

Ramsay Street, Coalsnaughton, before redevelopment in the 1950s.

Village Hall

Rankine

rows built by Robert Bald, the enlightened Alloa mining engineer.

Left: Coalsnaughton Hall.
Above: Leishman's original design.
Below: Aberdona House.

101 **Coalsnaughton Public Hall and Library,** John S. Leishman (Alloa), 1907; William Kerr, 1925
A low pink-harled, rambling complex of slate-roofed community buildings, the doorways well marked with relevant titles, and Tudor-like gabled parapets. Kerr's lesser hall has typical square bay windows with overhanging hipped eaves.

RCAHMS

Aberdona House, from 18th century
Set in extensive grounds east of Gartmorn Dam, this enchanting group of buildings comprises an early 18th century wing to the north, and a mid-18th century wing to the east, joined together c. 1860 at the south-west angle by a tall three-storey Tudor tower complete with battlements. It retains many 18th century fittings. The house was built by the Erskines of Alva, and became part of Harviestoun Estate (of which it is now the principal residence) about 1860.

Harviestoun Castle (demolished)
Harviestoun, now commemorated by gate lodges, stables and the Home Farm, was blown up in 1970.

Robert Burns visited Harviestoun on at least two occasions during 1787, to see his friend Gavin Hamilton, Burns recorded: *After breakfast we made a party to go and see the Cauldron Linn: a remarkable cascade in the Devon about five miles from Harviestoun; and after spending one of the most pleasant days I ever had in my life, I returned to Stirling in the evening.* Burns' pleasure was probably caused by Mrs Hamilton's daughter Charlotte, to whom Burns wrote his poem *The Banks of the Devon.*

The Banks of the Devon
*How pleasant the banks of the
    clear winding Devon,
With green-spreading bushes, and
    flow'rs blooming fair!
But the bonniest flow'r on the
    banks of the Devon
Was once a sweet bud on the braes
    of the Ayr.*

*Let Bourbon exult in his gay,
    gilded Lilies,
And England triumphant display
    her proud Rose;
A fairer than either adorns the
    green vallies
Where Devon, sweet Devon,
    meandering flows.*

Burns' last poem, written nine days before he died in 1796, was *Fairest Maid on Devon Banks,* the maid being Charlotte's cousin Margaret (Peggy) Chambers.

*Fairest maid on Devon banks,
Chrystal Devon, winding Devon,
Wilt thou lay that frown aside,
And smile as thou wert wont to do?*

HARVIESTOUN

John Tait, a wealthy Edinburgh lawyer, had bought *a tolerably good house* on the old high road in 1780. His son Craufurd, who succeeded in 1800, was the principal mover in the matter of the new Turnpike Road from Stirling to Kinross. The latter improved both house and estate, demolishing the original hamlets on the road. The stretch of the new Turnpike at Harviestoun was designed with curves following the River Devon to provide changing views through the valley. He also created a beautiful garden around the mansion using, according to his daughter, Milton's description of the garden of Eden as his guide. It had wild water and formal gardens and a burn running through a cave (incorporating a 1610 datestone) descending over a small waterfall to a pool. Tait introduced agricultural and mechanical innovations to the estate, one example being a mechanical spit in the kitchen, powered by water from the Harviestoun Burn.

Harviestoun Castle.

The Stable Block, late 18th century, is U-shaped in plan, fronted by a long, classical ashlar block, a pediment above an arched pend at the centre. The extensive **Home Farm,** c. 1820, comprises a two-storey E-plan steading with cart-arches, crowsteps and classical mouldings, dominated by a fine octagonal tower with stone spire. A small, but grand farmhouse sits at each side of the steading, each with an elegant pyramidal roof topped by an endearing group of four central chimneys. **The East and West Lodges** are tiny battlemented versions of the Castle. At the East Lodge is a small commemorative cairn to Robert Burns. A private coal mine still operates within the estate. **Tait's Tomb,** the small burial ground of the Taits of Harviestoun, is within the high circular stone wall at a sharp bend in the main road.

Sheardale House, c. 1855 (demolished)
Built on the north face of Sheardale Ridge by John Millar, a retired Edinburgh china merchant, the last occupants of the house were said to run through icy halls wearing overcoats. **Wester Sheardale,** 18th century, is an L-shaped steading, with an outside stair to the lofts above the arched carriage doorway, a heraldic panel, and a large walled kitchen garden behind. It is presently being restored and renovated by Peter Allam. **Sheardale Village** comprises a number of attractive slated or pantiled cottages of the 18th and 19th century lining the Sheardale Road.

102

CDC Tech Services

Castle Campbell, 15th century onward

Set high above Dollar on a natural eminence, guarded by steep ravines on three sides, Castle Campbell was the chief lowland stronghold of the Earls of Argyll. The tower, dating from the 15th century, is the oldest and best preserved section of the castle, now entered through a later arched loggia in the east range. A south range of principal apartments was added c. 1500, with a large fireplace, and south facing windows, above a row of cellars. An octagonal stair tower to the west, and square tower to the east led to an upper floor. The splendid, palace-like east range was built c. 1600, faced by an elegant ashlar screen wall. An unusual loggia is formed by arches supported on moulded columns, behind which are two vaulted chambers with moulded ribs — similar to those of the top room of the tower.

Colin Campbell, 1st Earl of Argyll, acquired the Castle (then known as Gloume), through his wife, an heiress of Walter Stewart of Lorne. During the centuries when the range of buildings around the tower were constructed, the Earls of Argyll held some of the highest positions in the land — ambassadors, Masters of the King's Household, Justiciar of Scotland, Lord High Chancellor of Scotland — and later the strong and constant supporters of the Protestant faith. It is likely that John Knox administered the Holy Sacrament for one of the first times during his visit to the Castle in 1556.

Lady Nairne, one of Scotland's best songwriters, must have had a relapse when visiting Castle Campbell:

O Castell Gloom! on thy fair wa's
Nae banners now are streamin',
The houlet flits amang thy ha's,
And wild birds there are screamin'.
Oh! mourn the woe, oh! mourn the crime,
Frae civil war that flows;
Oh! mourn, Argyle, thy fallen line,
And mourn the great Montrose.

Top: Castle Campbell.
Left: Aerial view.

RCAHMS

Billings' engraving of the top chambers of the tower, c. 1850; the floor is now reinstated.

The Castle ceased to be a great stronghold around the mid 17th century; it is supposed that General Monk destroyed it in 1654. On a clear day, the view from the tower is one of the finest in Scotland; when cloudy, enclosed by rolling banks of mist, there is a sense of awe-inspiring isolation and timelessness. Open to the public; guide book available.

Dollar Glen

An enchanting and exhilarating walk past deep gorges and high waterfalls amid an abundant plant life growing on the wooded slopes. The paths continue above the Castle and have been owned and maintained by the National Trust for Scotland since 1953.

The Old Town of Dollar

Although the first reference to Dollar parish is in the Dark Ages, it figures little in early history. It was utterly burnt in 1645 as part of an attack upon the Earl of Argyll and Castle Campbell. The first visible remains of pre-Academy Dollar is the village formed around the burn and Argyll's grain mill at the head of Mill Green (which was created as a public bleachfield by the Duke in the 18th century not long before Argyll sold the estate to Craufurd Tait of Harviestoun). In 1800 the first woollen mill was built, and the harled stone building at the North Bridge was 103 **Brunt Mill,** which succeeded it in 1822, ceasing in 1837, later preserved by the Harviestoun Estate for *the amenity of Dollar.*

Pre-Academy Dollar is now called the *Old Town,* to the east of North Bridge. It was never a substantial community; so insignificant, indeed, that Robert Forsyth thought it merited no mention in 1804 in his *Beauties of Scotland.* Garnett, travelling through a few years earlier from Dunfermline to Stirling, recorded *a small village with a wretched Inn. Although well situated for an Inn, it is unfortunate that there is not a house which would afford tolerable accommodation for travellers.*

A romanticised mid 19th century impression of Dollar from Burnside.

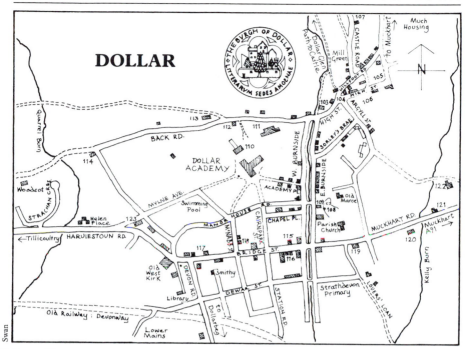

DOLLAR

¹⁰⁴**Cross Keys**

The heart of the Old Town is the sloping square facing the Cross Keys from which Argyll Street leads south, High Street to the east and west, and Hillfoot Road to the north-east. **Cross Keys House, 1-3 Hillfoot Road,** is a former 18th century Drovers' Inn now converted into houses: a wide, five-window house with crowstepped gables, **No. 1** has a rustic porch and a basement (once a beer cellar) below. **No. 3** was restored by Duncan Stirling in 1975.

The Village Store, 1806, was one of the grandest buildings in Dollar at the time of building, with its scrolled skewputts, architrave above the door, well proportioned windows and re-used 18th century datestone. The emblem of a horse rearing above the door is that of the Scottish Union Fire Insurance.

High Street

Mainly lined with cottages of 1800-40 vintage, many of which were feued by the Duke of Argyll in 1807. Note the quaint **Priory** with its gabled dormer windows (the sandstone rubble box in the garage behind being a former 1860 Mission Hall); the pantile, rubble-built cottages further up; **Southview** dated 1799, white harled, two-storey to the rear and pantiled with slate apron like its neighbour, No. 34, **Baldinnes.** The street level entrance of **The Luggy,**

The Village Store.

Dollar Academy

Swan

Top: Dollar Old Town in 1907.
Above: Moss Court, High Street
— a blend of old and new.

the eastmost house, conceals a former byre below.
105 **Moss Court** and **Brewlands Court** are modern
106 Scots rendered with cement margins and small
windows.

Hillfoot Road
Narrow and steeply winding, note **The Aikars** (No.
11), a white 18th century cottage distinguished by its
rolled skewputts; **Broomieknowe Cottage,** a grander
two-storey version, in whinstone; the diminutive one
door, one window, **Cashmere Cottage; Glenview,**
whose basement was once a butcher's, and retains its
ceiling meathooks and bottle glass windows; the fine
whinstone **The Broomieknowe** and **The Knowe;**
early 19th century, with its odd *cherry-cocking* between
the larger pilastered doorway and hipped dormer
windows.

The Tower, 1867, Peter Sinclair
A large Scottish baronial house, surrounded by tall
cypresses, entered through a turreted tower decorated
with thistle-shaped motifs, finials and ornate rope-
design string courses. The old Muckhart back road
continues up the hill, a hillside now dominated by
rows of closely spaced speculative housing, forming an
almost isolated commuter-town, built from the
mid-1960s — to accommodate managerial staff from
the industrial Central Belt attracted to the school —
with little thought to the traffic implications for the
old town.

Hillfoot House, drawn by Colin
Gibson.

Hillfoot House, c. 1900 (demolished)
Stone, harled and turreted, it was large and high but
lacked any real architectural character. The estate,
which belonged to the Drysdales, was landscaped and
planted with exotic trees many of which survive.

Castle Road was the drove road through Glenquey
to Glendevon and Auchterarder, with a less adequate

RCAHMS

path through the hills to Blackford. For many years the villages on either side of the Ochils traded with each other via such hill roads. **No. 1** was built by Andrew Sharp as his smithy and dwellinghouse in the late 18th century. The little pyramid-roofed structure nearby was the hydraulic ram which served the Victorian Water Works. **Blinkbonny,** 1797, the last cottage, is set at an angle to the road, secluded within a private garden. An attractive whitewashed house with attic dormers and plain margins, painted around the windows, it was extended cleverly to the rear by Colin Campbell, 1973. **No. 19,** by David Wallace, 1968, is a large L-plan brick house with a flat roof, the double-storey living room is set into the hillside below the remainder of the accommodation.

Castle Road.

Argyll Street
The last principal street of the Old Town, mostly redeveloped save for two small cottages and the refaced **Lorne Tavern. Sorley's Brae** was built by a weaver (John Sorley), the most notable being **Nos. 14/16,** a long pantiled single-storey cottage of the late 18th century,

East Burnside
A special feature of Dollar is the burn, its banks favourite sitting places of people resting on a summer's day, its verges and boulders ideal for children's nature studies and for guddling small trout. To each side of its cherry tree-lined banks are fine late Georgian and Victorian cottages and villas. **Argyll Cottage,** c. 1800 (No. 6), is a Georgian fronted cottage, the attic with canted dormers, the door surround splayed, and front windows in V-plan bays.

The Mylne or **Middle Bridge** is a flat segmented stone arch, reputedly built c. 1820 to enable the Rev. Andrew Mylne, first Rector of the Academy, to walk between the School and the Church and Manse.

Below: Argyll Cottage.
Bottom: East Burnside.

108 The Auld Kirk, 1775

Prominent on the ridge above this delightful part of the town, sits the ruined gable and empty belfry of the roofless Auld Kirk. It replaced a more ancient church on a nearby site, from which came the 17th century belfry. The Kirkyard contains some fine late 18th and 19th century memorials, the older ones said to have been *borrowed* by the Minister for supporting his hayricks in the nearby glebe.

109 The Old School House, 1780

A big rubble block with pantile roof, and a small gabled porch. It replaced the original 1640 school and continued to serve as a parish school for the next century. Now used as the Session House, it was re-roofed in 1982. **The Burnside Hall**, a large rectangular Gothic church with a broach spire, was built for the United Presbyterians in 1876 by Neil Macara.

Top: The Auld Kirk and Kirkyard — one stone bears the single legend *this stone keeps to the dyke.*
Right: The Old School House.
Below: Park House.

West Burnside has a few late Georgian houses, the ones nearer Bridge Street built with shops. **Chapel Place** was formerly a cul-de-sac off Cairnpark Street. **Park House**, 1822, is a fine Georgian house with a Doric pilastered doorpiece and well sculpted skewputts.

Swan

Dollar Academy.

Turnpike and the Academy

In 1806, the new road from Kinross to Stirling offered the Taits of Harviestoun the chance of feuing a series of large houses facing it. Some of those houses, built from the 1820s, remain as **Bridge Street.** The focus of the village was dragged south; a new Dollar was in the making (letting the old one slumber away peacefully uphill); a more economic, enlightened 19th century Dollar was symbolised by the new Academy.

Dollar Academy, 1818-20, William Playfair
The Trustees appointed one of Scotland's finest architects, and he responded by creating on the sloping ground to the west of the burn, an educational colony of a grandeur fully worthy of its dramatic setting. It consists of a splendid south-west facing facade of two-storeys, dominated by a giant pedimented portico at the head of a flight of stairs, and flanked by pilastered wings. The Doric style was that normally symbolic of high-quality learning. The principal room inside was the splendid Greek-Ionic colonnaded library — perhaps a precursor of the Upper Library in Edinburgh University: but that,

Dollar Academy was founded on the munificence of a former herd boy from Dollar, John McNabb (b. 1732), who became a wealthy sea captain resident in East London. He died in 1802 leaving half his fortune (worth £74,000 by 1818), *for the endowment of a charity or school for the poor of the parish of Dollar* under the control of the Kirk Session. Such a scale of endowment to a parish of 670 souls, caused considerable problems. Only after the Minister died in 1815, and replaced by the Rev. Andrew Mylne, was a school determined upon; and in 1837, almost 20 years later, Robert Chambers could write (though not without bias) that *the Academy has ultimately in a great measure failed, partly through a series of indecorous squabbles occasioned by the irresponsible power with which its management was entrusted and partly on account of the dislike of persons in the middle and superior walks of life to allow their children to mingle with the less carefully trained urchins of the village.* Six years later, such problems were at an end. It was the school which attracted attention, its 212 scholars, about a seventh of the entire population of the parish which had over-doubled in size since 1802, caused by *the flocking of strangers to reside in the village for the sake of the excellent means of education it held out.*

Dollar Academy

Left: The Playfair Library, c. 1930.

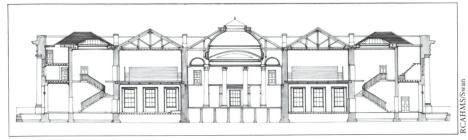

Section through Dollar Academy, original Playfair drawing.

RCAHMS/Swan

along with the rest of the interior, was lost in a fire which gutted the building in 1960. The interior was recast by Watson, Salmond and Gray in 1962 in a more utilitarian mould, creating three storeys where before there were two, a gymnasium and school hall carved from the 1866 wing at the rear. Several new buildings have been added to the policies, which are still enclosed by a low stone wall, a gateway at each drive.

110 **Science and Domestic Building,** 1910, Sir Rowand Anderson and Paul (later extended)
A pleasant neo-classical block whose projecting gabled entrance reaching through both storeys encloses a door flanked by Ionic pilasters.

Below: Science and Domestic Building.
Bottom: 3 Academy Place.
Bottom right: McNabb Street drive gateway.

111 **Preparatory School,** William Kerr, 1937
A long classroom block with red-tile hipped roof, large windows to the south, clerestory lighting to the north.

Academy Place, William Playfair, 1820-30
Six classical houses built for the Academy as Masters' accommodation flanking the original entrance from the east. All ashlar fronted in Playfair's more rustic vein, the roofs hipped with shallow pitches, the two western houses having central chimneys, and the overhanging eaves supported by modillion brackets. Each door is graced with a triangular pediment supported on unusual notched brackets.

Swan

Swan

Swan

The Back Road

The Academy is bounded along its northern perimeter by the old high road from Stirling to Kinross, open to the hills beyond until enclosed by 20th century developments. **Glenvar** (No. 4), by William Kerr, 1908, an unusual gabled villa of harled brickwork, has the steep double gabled roofs over tall bay windows, corner verandah and conservatory reminiscent of English Arts and Crafts buildings. The arched recessed porch, tall stair oriel window, and tiny side round window make an impressive western entrance. **Meadowbank** (No. 8), also by William Kerr (similar

Glenvar.

Meadowbank.

to Glenvar in form), was designed for the same family some 30 years on (1934). Behind the north Academy gate (formerly a carriage entrance) was the heather-
112 thatched **Gardener's Cottage**, 1820. Now with a slate roof, and used by the Army Cadets, the cottage is a charming example of a small Georgian gate lodge with projecting doorway.

113 **Brooklyn,** c. 1870
A large four-villa terrace of masters' houses, each half-villa with a projecting gable, cast-iron entrance verandah and round-headed windows. **28 Back Road,** 1960, is an intriguing and unusual house in flat-roofed red brick designed by Alastair Milne.
114 **Thornbank Cottage,** mid 19th century, is an early example of such Gothic villas with projecting gable and bay window.

Above: 28 Back Road.
Left: Brooklyn.

Gateside is an ancient estate, an old charter stipulating that the feuholder must present a passing monarch with ale: five gallons each of old brewed ale, new ale, and ale in the process of brewing. In the 18th century, it was the principal Inn serving travellers passing along the old road. The house brewed its own beer until the early 19th century, the water coming from a spring in Brewer's Knowe behind.

Right: Bridge Street.

Top: 86 Bridge Street.
Above: 88/90 Bridge Street, built in the Thirties by Hutchison of Kinross.

Bridge Street
The Clydesdale Bank, Bridge Street east, 1870s
A typical Italianate banking palazzo, with triple and coupled windows, elaborate doorway, bracketed eaves and low hipped roof. One of the first villas feued by the Taits was **Homefield,** c. 1822, a fine house with a front of droved ashlar, the architraved door enhanced by ornamental rosettes, a decoration repeated on other doors in the street.

Rosevale, 1820s
Symmetrical, well-proportioned windows with their original glazing bars, a central door flanked by pilasters, the whole composition tied together by a cornice at eaves line, and well set off by a tidy front garden. No. 86 is another good example of the 1820s feuing.

Waddell's has notable Victorian shop fronts and fittings. **Dewar House,** an Academy Boarding House (formerly Aberdona) and **Freshfields,** at the corner of Devon Road, are a pair of Tudor-gabled, double-villas of the 1850s, with neat gabled porches and ground floor bay windows.

Victorian Expansion
The obvious development after Bridge Street was built to extend northwards towards the Academy.
Cairnpark Street was developed first, feued by the Academy in the 1830s, and comprises a simple double-sided street of terraced cottages, forming a pleasant group looking past the Academy to the Castle and hills. **Speedwell,** 13 McNabb Street, c. 1820, is a simple classical house with a low pitched roof, decorated with a wooden ornamental apron.

South of the Main Road
The opening of the railway in 1869 brought Stirling within only 20 minutes reach, and the line to Kinross

was soon to be joined at Rumbling Bridge, opening up Dollar to the east. The old railway line — now a country walk — still forms the southern boundary of the town. **Station Road,** lower **McNabb Street** and **Devon Road** (the main Dunfermline Road), all projected downwards from the main road and during the 1870s, 80s and 90s were built up with small, one-storey cottages. **Dewar Street,** which forms the horizontal of the grid, has a fine row of 1870s cottages with canted dormers. The early 19th century **Smithy** in Campbell Street, still in operation as such, provides a tall brick chimney, rising above this low weather-beaten brick building, as a landmark.

The Smithy.

Sir James Dewar (1842-1923), a native of Kincardine, was educated at Dollar Academy. His invention of the vacuum flask was necessary to his discovery (with Sir Fredrick Able) of cordite. He is recollected by Dewar House and Street.

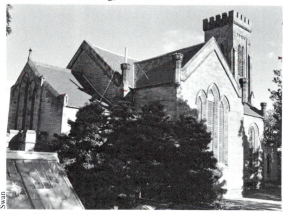

Muckhart Road
Dollar Parish Church, Sir William Tite, 1841 Cruciform Gothic, dominated by the tall, battlemented bell-tower at the south end. At each corner of the roof is a small corbelled angle turret with a crenellated top. The old **Manse,** St Columba's House, is a huge rambling building, originally a three-window house of 1795, enlarged by Rev. A. Mylne in 1817. The tiny **Kirkyard Keeper's Cottage,** c. 1840, has a central doorway with wooden porch and neat piended slate
119 roof. **Seberham** was built, c. 1820, for one of the first masters of the Academy, with a wide-eaved piended roof, canted dormer windows and unusually
120 sculpted chimney shafts. **The Pines,** 1938, by William Kerr with Patrick McNeil, with Scots vernacular inspired detailing, is an excellent example of the contemporary desire to be both modern and Scots. A simply projecting stair tower, a Venetian bedroom window, and an elegant stone carved door
121 form the north-facing entrance. **Burnbrae Lodge,** early 19th century, built as **The Oak Coaching Inn,** is distinguished by its fine Doric, columned porchway.
122 **Kellyside,** by William Kerr, 1905, is a large mansion, early English in style, with mock half-timbered gables and sweeping red-tile roof.

Left: Dollar Parish Church.
Below: The Pines.

G

Harviestoun Road
Former **West Free Church,** 1859
A large Gothic church (now split into two houses) which contains an early example of laminated timber beams in its roof structure, and incorporates rainwater downpipes within internal columns.

Library (Jersey House), Henderson Place, 1876
A dog-tooth pattern brick villa built by the Manager of the Dollar Brickworks as an advertisement for his product.

Swan

Right: St James the Great.
Below: The Rectory.
Bottom: Helen Place.

123 **St James the Great** (Episcopal), Adam Frame, 1879-82
A small Gothic nave and chancel designed in the Early English Gothic often adopted by the Episcopalians as being nearer to their uncompromised roots. The **Rectory** (built as Viewfield, c. 1830) is strictly classical with a Doric pilastered door and matching side wings.

Swan

Helen Place, c. 1830
Three single-storey and basement houses around a courtyard, the middle house at the rear faithfully restored. It is a refronting of a late 18th century Brewer's House: a simple ashlar cottage with a hipped roof, the window rybats are picked out in white sandstone and the door surrounded by a wide raised entablature.

Swan

Western Approach
The western approach to Dollar is lined by large neo-classical houses built for the Academy's first masters who were learned and often wealthy scholars head-hunted to bring prestige to the Academy.

Woodcot, c. 1845
1950s Mactaggart and Mickel suburb (which perpetuates 1930s details and imagery with corner windows) built in its parkland, Woodcot is a good

example of a late Georgian cottage: ashlar front, Doric-pilastered entrance flanked by windows, the arrangement of the segmental fanlight and door side lights identical to nearby Helen Place.

124 **Springfield,** c. 1830, has two-storey bay windows flanking a pilastered entrance. It has a twin nearby: **Strathdevon.**

125 **Devongrove,** 1821, possibly William Playfair
An elegant mansion with projecting centre, screen side wings, hipped roof; a segmented fanlight sits above an entrance flanked by Doric pilasters, and the ground floor windows are within arched recesses like nearby **Birchgrove,** c. 1750.

126 **Broomrigg,** from 1804
Two-storey, stucco-faced Italianate, recast c. 1890 with double bow windows, balustraded, wall finials, parapet and a double-columned porch. The mahogany fitted library was built by craftsmen from the then owner's shipyard on the Clyde. On the roadside is an early 19th century fountain — a cast-iron boy with pitcher within a rock-faced dome.

Mount Devon, 1827
A classical house, the ground floor is rusticated ashlar, with a Doric-columned porch. Screen wings added in 1847 complete the composition.

127 **The Horseshoe,** an 1830s Tudor cottage with a central stone gable, was built as the Factor's House to Harviestoun Estate.

Lower Mains
A hamlet comprising a few tidy cottages and neat Council housing. The principal building is **Ochilton House,** Devon Road, a 19th century house with a hexagonal porch.

William Tennant (1784-1848) is remembered as the author of *Anster Fair* (1812), the mock heroic poem describing his native Anstruther market. He came to Dollar in 1819 as the classics teacher and built Devongrove. A cripple from childhood, he *used two crutches and had a long walk daily to school.* In 1834 he left the Academy to become Professor of Oriental Languages at St Mary's College, St Andrews. Captain Charles Gray (1782-1851), expert on Scottish song, attempted to commemorate his co-founder of the *Anstruther Mousomanik Society* thus:
Thy river, clear winding, flows softly along,
Like the music of verse, or the notes of a song;
There the trout in his pastime glides swift as a dart,
And oft cheats the angler, though crafty his art;
There the tenants of nature at freedom may rove,
No gun, net or link lurks in sweet Devongrove.

Above left: Devongrove.
Above: Broomrigg.

Dollarbeg.

128 **Dollarfield**

In 1783 William Haig founded commercial bleachworks along the north bank of the River Devon, to bleach cloth for the Dunfermline linen trade. It lasted until the middle of this century. The site is now a caravan park. **Dollarfield House**, the Haigs' mansion, was destroyed by fire in 1940 and replaced by a modern farmhouse. The original steading, now considerably altered, was once the largest continuous lofted steading in Scotland. The Dairy, or West Range, hosts the small **Harviestoun Brewery.** Across the Bridge the **Rackmill** was a Waulk, or beading, mill in use about 1800.

Dollarbeg, Ebenezer Simpson, c. 1900
A rambling, ornate red sandstone baronial mansion on an ancient site high on the south ridge above Dollar. A fruit salad of embellishment: corbelled turrets, crowstepped gables, moulded string courses, arched entrance porch and a high four-storey entrance tower, similarly decorated. Contemporary stables, and a suitably turreted and crowstepped gate lodge.

OPPOSITE:
Above: Vicar's Bridge in 1902.
Below: Muckhart Mill, the wheel is now working.

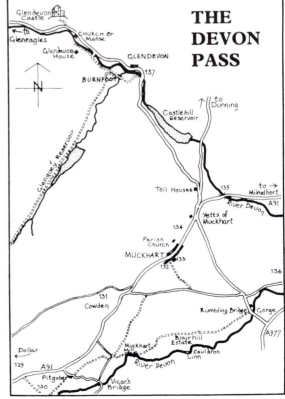

THE
DEVON
PASS

East of Dollar

129 **Kellybank** is a well-proportioned, early 19th century farmhouse. In the 19th century coal mines and lime kilns were developed here, and at neighbouring **Middleton,** and traces of the mill wheel on the Kelly Burn which drove the mine shaft pump may still be seen.

130 **Wester Pitgober** comprises two adjoining farmhouses, the east wing a two-storey, rubble house, c. 1790, and the main house c. 1850 a traditional three-window, two-storey block, featuring an unusual re-used armorial panel.

Dollar Academy

Muckhart Mill, from 1666
The site of some building (and the local grain mill powered by the Hole Burn) since the 14th century, the mill comprises three different rubble pantiled buildings set together at uneven angles. Its main feature is the cast-iron overshot waterwheel whose diameter of 20 ft makes it one of the largest wheels in Scotland. **The Mill House and Steading,** 1780, is tall, whitewashed and pantiled. A huge 35 ft disused lime kiln, with three arched openings, is built into the cliff face nearby. The ancient rubble bridge over the Hole Burn has a masonic evil eye to ward off unwelcome spirits.

Cowden Castle

About 1320, Bishop William Lamberton of St Andrews built a fortified palace known as Castleton, and some form of mansion remained here until a new house was built in 1834. Ruins at Cowden consist of an octagonal turret, c. 1800, with a 1707 re-used lintel, and a 16th century moulded entrance arch, both incorporated in a crenellated wall of c. 1800. The old **Stables** nearby have been converted into a house. An interesting Victorian arch leading to the ruins is topped by an 18th century bellcote with fluted pilasters and ball finials. This house was enlarged and remodelled in 1893 by Honeyman and Keppie for John Christie (demolished 1952).

Vicar's Bridge

Early photographs show an enchanting single-arched bridge, entranced by its own reflection in the Devon, which collapsed in the 1950s and was replaced by a piece of modern utility. A bridge was erected on this site in the 16th century. A 1765 plaque tells us *Thomas Forrest, who among other acts of charity, built this bridge.* Forrest was the *Good Vicar of Dollar,* a martyr of the Reformation who, choosing to preach by the Bible, was burnt for his beliefs in 1539 following his attendance at Thomas Cocklaw's wedding. Forrest chose a beautiful setting for his bridge, to the advantage of the modern day picnic area, which has recently been revitalised by the District Council. An old oak tree nearby has the initials J B cut into its bark. In 1865 Joseph Bell attacked a baker, travelling on the lonely road, was found guilty of murder and was given the last public execution in Scotland in Perth.

CDC Tech Services

A number of mines and kilns left over from lime and ironstone workings of the early 19th century can be discovered in the locality of Vicar's Bridge. In 1830 the water draining out of one of the disused mine entrances was found to contain sufficient chemicals to be the attributed cure for a staggering number and variety of diseases.

COWDEN

The leader of the Antiburgher section of the Scottish Secession Church, **Adam Gibb** (1714-1788), came from Cowden (then known as Castleton). The Antiburghers (1747) believed it unlawful that city burgesses (magistrates) should have to take an oath to *the true religion presently professed within this realm.*

Ian Campbell

The Japanese Gardens during one of its last public openings in the 1950s.

131 **The Japanese Garden,** Ella Christie and Taki Honda, 1907
The lifelong home of Ella Christie, an intrepid traveller who travelled to Europe, India, Tibet, China, Japan, Malaya, Burma, North Africa and America. After visiting Japan in 1907 she decided to transform a marshy field at Cowden into a Japanese Garden. With the help of Taki Honda, a Japanese lady gardener, and the advice of Professor Susuki, Head of Soani School of Imperial Design (who thought it *the best garden in the western world),* she laid out a lake surrounded by trees and shrubs, stepping stones and shrines with islands and bridges. From 1925, the garden had the caring attention of Mr Matsou, a Japanese gardener who had lost all his family in an earthquake. Matsou died in 1936 and is buried in Muckhart Churchyard. Ella died in 1948 and the family were unable to maintain Cowden and the garden; nor were they able to interest anyone else. The shrines were vandalised, the tea houses burnt down, and new trees planted round about. Fortunately many of the trees survived and matured. It was the only large-scale Japanese Garden in Britain and was much frequented by Andrew Lang (1844-1912), poet, scholar, author and above all, great eccentric, during his last years.

Muckhart
Frequent winner of *Scotland's best kept village* title for its flowing beds of colour, and profusion of hanging baskets and window boxes, Muckhart guards the Glendevon pass through the Ochils to Perthshire from the counties of Kinross (to the east), Fife (to the south), and Clackmannan (to the west). The outlying cottages, near the road junction, are known as the *Yetts of Muckhart* (*Yett* meaning gate); whereas the body of the village is the *Pool.* The village owes its existence to the drove road through the Pass, and in

the last century it was common for at least every other cottage to become a hostelry around market time. The village has expanded little beyond the original street of low stone cottages.

The Inn.

The Inn, 1806, is a double white-rendered cottage with black margins, a pantiled roof and a slate easing course, generally typical of Muckhart cottages. The wooden oriel windows are a modern touch, but go well with the picturesqueness of the village. **The**
132 **Coronation Hall,** 1911, imported from the Glasgow Exhibition, is a white harled brick chamber.
Dungloe, is a half-timbered English villa with a wide west-facing verandah. The nearby houses, in **School Road,** are the typical 1950s County Architect cottages. Two steep-roofed 1946 double-houses clad in vertical boarding by Ian Moodie, in Swedish style, are just as charming. The cottages along the **Main Road** all date from around the early 1800s, each delighting in an arcadian name: *Ochil House, Woodend, Hillview,*
133 *Ivy Cottage.* **Hollytree Lodge** is grander with its tripartite doorway and fanlight, similar to houses on the outskirts of Dollar.

Hollytree Lodge.

Parish Church, 1838
A simple rubble chamber with small square bellcote and fine Georgian arched windows. Original woodwork in the pews and west gallery. Set into the east gable are four datestones representing previous churches on the site: 1620, 1699, 1713 and 1789, above a memorial to the Christies of Cowden. The nearby Manse, 1832-34, by William Stirling, is a fairly
134 plain, traditional, two-storey house. **Balliliesk,** late 19th century, is an Italianate house with an extra

CDC Tech Services

storey in the squat tower, a fine conservatory range, a walled garden and related offices. **Ellislea**, at Yetts of Muckhart, late 18th century, is a good house with a fine rectangular fanlight. Both quoins and door dressings are unusually finished with a bold rustication.

Fossoway

An ancient parish now largely made up of the villages of **Drum** and **Crook of Devon** in Kinross-shire. 135 **North Fossoway Bridge,** carrying the Milnathort road over the River Devon, is a single segmental arch of great antiquity, repaired in 1780, and again in 1882 — the date it bears.

136 **Lendrickmuir School,** 1874, is an impressive, unorthodox, neo-classical mansion designed by Adam Frame for Robert Moubray of Cambus Distillery, as Naemoor House. The interior includes very elaborate plasterwork.

Top: Hallway, Lendrickmuir.
Right: Rumbling Bridge.

Rumbling Bridge and Devon Gorge

Beside the Old Coaching Inn (c. 1790 and now a nursing home) is one of the most beautiful stretches of the River Devon.

At Rumbling Bridge the water has cut deep through the landscape to form gorges, pools and waterfalls. As the taste for romantic experience grew, the Devon Gorge was added to the list of sights. In 1769 Thomas Pennant made a detour to admire *the large and deep cylindrical cavities like cauldrons. One in particular has the appearance of a vast brewing vessel; and the water, by its great agitation, has acquired a yellow scum exactly resembling the yeasty working of a malt liquor.* Sarah Murray, in 1798 advised all travellers to divert for the thrill and, in the 19th century, they did. Coaches travelling from Edinburgh to the Highlands made regular stops at Rumbling Bridge Hotel. In 1871 the railway was joined by the **Devon Valley Railway** providing five of the most beautiful miles of railway in the country, under and over 17 bridges and a viaduct, close to the banks of the river. **Rumbling Bridge Station,** to which visitors flocked in their thousands, survives as housing.

Swan

Rumbling Bridge, 1713 and 1864
The old lower bridge, only 12 ft wide without parapets, was built by William Gray. The bridge above was superimposed 150 years later creating an unusual double bridge. Viewed from below, it is a spectacular sight, and the reverberating sounds of the river forcing its way through the rocks explain its name. The **Devil's Mill,** the loudest of the cascades producing noise like running machinery, never ceases even on the Sabbath; and thus earned its title. The celebrated **Walks** have been re-opened with new bridges, gates and access points. Leaflet available.

The Cauldron Linn, is said to be one of the finest waterfalls in Scotland. Between two falls, which together total about 90 ft, are three deep pools, or linns, gouged out of the rock. The water flows through holes under the surface, and the froth on the surface of each pool makes them resemble witches' cauldrons. Of **Blairhill,** an estate linked to the Haig whisky family, only the estate cottages and lodges survive; the immense walled garden has been repossessed by nature and a small family shrine is shrouded in dense woodland.

Up the Glendevon Road are two former **Toll Houses** flanking each side of the road by the Dunning junction. The west is unaltered: three windows, with a broad-eaved, hipped roof and centre chimney.

Glendevon
The new **Castlehill Reservoir,** on the River Devon, has flooded the valley alongside the road. **St Serf's Bridge,** an ancient single arch with, some say,

Swan

Above: Cauldron Linn.
Below: The eastern Toll House.
Bottom: Castlehill Reservoir.

Swan

Swan

GLENDEVON

Right: The old Castle Hotel.

Swan

Below: Glendevon Church in 1899.
Centre: Glendevon House.
Bottom: Glendevon Castle.

RCAHMS

Swan

RIAS Library

137 monastic carvings below, was the loss. The old **Castle Hotel** has been stripped of its Victorian castellations and now, behind the great entrance arch, is a simple villa with Italianate campanile. The **Tormaukin,** still a pleasant hotel, was a 19th century coaching inn, with earlier memories of sheep droving days.

Burnfoot, a deserted weaving hamlet on the other side of the river by the Glenquey Burn, is survived by a few stone cottages and a sturdy arched bridge.

Glendevon House, probably by Gillespie Graham, c. 1830, is a very fine neo-Tudor cottage house, with a low-pitched broad-eaved roof; and an arched gateway — with a 1766 panel associated with the Castle — and lodge by the river. **Glendevon Church,** in the shadows of the immense Scots **Manse,** is a simple 1803 whitewashed chamber with five rectangular windows, a square stone bellcote and a plain slate roof: who could want more in these beautiful surroundings?

Glendevon Castle, 15th century onwards
Formerly Z-plan, only the four-storey south tower survives full height, the north tower and main block being reduced in height and considerably altered. The first castle on the site belonged to the Douglas family in the 15th century, from which part of the massive central block may date, being extended to Z-plan in the early 17th century, possibly when it passed to the Rutherfords. Now a wayside hostelry.

ACKNOWLEDGEMENTS

Many people have helped in the compilation of this book, pre-eminently Charles McKean, who enhanced and edited the text, and Stewart Fowler, who assisted throughout the project. I am indebted to the following — many of whom have read the text — for their assistance and suggestions: David Walker, Robert Rankine, Jean Peacock, Murray Dickie, Ronald Hunter, Duncan Stirling, Bill Bracewell, Vicki Bryant, Alex McLaren, Isobel Drummond, Rena Cowper, Isobel Stewart, Mary Kerr, Tony Martin, David Graham, Jennifer Campbell, Tom Jack, Peter Allam, Alan Wightman, and Lord Balfour of Burleigh. I also wish to acknowledge David Hynd and the staff of Clackmannan District Libraries; and especially thank Alison Ewart and Catherine Schroder at Greenfield House, and Tayona McKeown at the R.I.A.S., for typing.

WORKS CONSULTED FOR THIS GUIDE

The District Libraries have published an excellent series of old and new local works of which it is possible to acknowledge only the more significant. A useful source of information has been the Local Collection of books, pamphlets, letters, and photographs — and the microfilm copies and indices of local newspapers — held at Alloa Library.

BIBLIOGRAPHY

Adamson, J.: *A Glimpse into the Past of Sauchie and Alloa*, 1981; Archibald, J.: *Alloa Sixty Years Ago*, 1911; Billings, R. W.: *The Baronial and Ecclesiastical Architecture of Scotland*, 1852; Brown, W. C.: *Clackmannanshire, A Guide to Historical Sources*, 1984; Cockburn, Lord: *Circuit Journeys*, 1888; Cowper, A. S.: *Sidelights on Alva History*, 1972; Crawford, J.: *Memorials of the Town and Parish of Alloa*, 1874; Crouther Gordon, T.: *The History of Clackmannan*, 1936, *A Short History of Alloa*, 1937; *The Dictionary of National Biography; The Dollar Magazine*, from 1902; Dollar Civic Trust: *Chap Book*, 1977; Drummond, A. I. R.: *Old Clackmannanshire*, 1953, unpublished thesis: *The Castellated and Domestic Architecture of Clackmannanshire and its Borders from the Mediaeval Period to the Year 1830;* Evans, E. J.: *Tillicoultry, a Centenary History*, 1972; Gibson, W.: *Reminiscences of Dollar, Tillicoultry, Etc.*, 1883; Groome, F. H.: *Ordnance Gazeteer of Scotland;* 1882-85; Hume, J. R.: *The Industrial Archaeology of Scotland*, 1976; Kirk, R.: *Historical Sketch of Tullibody*, 1890 and 1937; Hume-Brown, P.: *Early Travellers in Scotland*, 1891; Lothian, J.: *Alloa and its Environs*, 1861; MacGibbon & Ross: *The Castellated and Domestic Architecture of Scotland*, 1887-92; McMaster, C.: *Alloa Ale*, 1985; Park, B. A.: *The Woollen Mill buildings in the Hillfoots Area*, 1979; Ramsay, J.: *Scotland and Scotsmen in the 18th century*, Allardyce edition, 1888; Scott, W.: *Waverley*, 1885 edition: S.D.D.: *Descriptive Lists of Buildings of Architectural and Historic Interest;* Wallace, J.: *The Sheriffdom of Clackmannan*, 1890; Watt, L.: *Alloa and Tullibody*, 1902; The First, Second and Third *Statistical Accounts.*

PHOTOGRAPHS

The source of each photograph is credited alongside. Particular thanks are due to Stewart Fowler, Alex McLaren, Anne Ferguson, the Royal Commission on the Ancient & Historic Monuments of Scotland, and Alloa Library. Paintings by David Allan are reproduced by kind permission of the Earl of Mar and Kellie, the Earl of Cathcart, and the University of Dundee. Their production owes much to White House Studios.

The support of Clackmannan District Council in the production of this guide is gratefully acknowledged.

Design by Dorothy Steedman.

CDC Libraries

An Ochils hill stream.

Blairdenon

Dumyat

Craig Leith

Myreton

Alva Glen

Silver Glen

ALVA
78

MENSTRIE
77

BLAIRLOGIE
72   73 74
A 91   76 Castle
75

to
Stirling

Glenochil
Yeast
Factory

River Devon

King o' Muirs

Old
Sauchie

Glenochil

Powis
to Stirling
A 907   Bridgend
Manor

69
TULLIBODY

70   67

71

Lornshill

SAUCHIE
66
67   Ho

Iron
Bridge   Distillery

CAMBUS

RIVER
FORTH

The
Gean   Inglewood

Arnsbrae

site of
Tullibody
House

ALLOA

LOOK ABOOT YE

CLACKMANNAN
DISTRICT

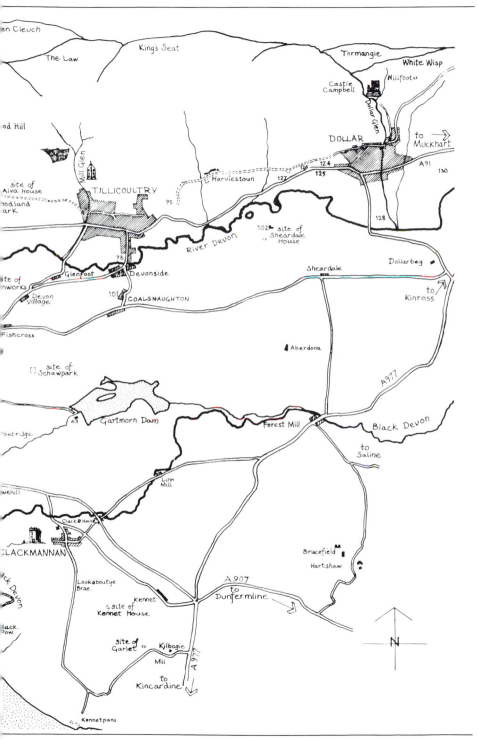

GLOSSARY

Architrave Moulding around a door or window; lowest part of entablature.

Art Nouveau Curvilinear decorative style popular c. 1890-1910.

Art and Crafts Movement of design, associated with William Morris, using handmade materials and English vernacular building and craft traditions.

Ashlar Evenly cut stone facing blocks.

Baroque Flamboyant architectural style that degenerated from the Italian Renaissance c. 1600.

Battlement Regular openings in parapet wall, originally as splayed gun-loops.

Bay window Any projecting window.

Bellcote Ornamental structure made to contain one or two bells, also **Belfry.**

Broach spire Spire in the form of a low square pyramid interpenetrated with a tall octagonal.

Bow window Curved projecting window.

Bracketed cornice Cornice with projecting supports.

Buttress Projecting structural support built onto the outside of a wall.

Calsie Paving, as in *causey stones.*

Campanile Detached tower, properly a bell-tower.

Canted window Projecting window with sloping sides.

Cap-house Small turretted structure at the top of a turnpike stair.

Capital The head of a classical column.

Castellations Battlements and turrets.

Channelled Grooved effect in stonework joints.

Cherry-cocking Small stones in the joints of larger stonework.

Classic Revival of classic architectural styles practised by ancient Greeks and Romans, distinguished by the column, entablature and pediment.

Clerestory Range of windows lighting the highest part of a tall room.

Collops Slices of meat.

Colonnade Range of evenly spaced columns.

Corbel Projecting structural support.

Corinthian Greek classical order, with *acanthus leaf* decorated capitals.

Cornice Projecting moulding along the top of a building, door, window, entablature, or edge of ceiling.

Crenellations Battlements.

Crowstep Step-like coping at head of gable, used where it was difficult to cut stone at an angle. From corbelled or *corbie-stane.*

Cupola Dome crowning a roof or turret.

Doric Greek classical order with undecorated capitals.

Eclecticism Selecting the *best* of other styles.

Entablature In classical architecture, the part between the columns and pediment, consisting of the architrave, frieze and cornice.

Entresol A low storey between two taller ones.

Finial Ornamental top to pinnacle, gable, etc.

Fluted Vertical grooves on a column.

Frotting Wearing down by rubbing.

Gargoyle Grotesquely carved projecting water spout.

Gothic Non-classical mediaeval architecture, distinguished by high-pitched roofs, sharp-pointed arches, and narrow windows, which progressively became less severe. Revived in its various forms by the Victorians: *Early English, Geometrical, Late Decorated, Perpendicular* or *Tudor.*

Groin vault Formed by two continuous vaults intersecting at right angles.

Hog-backed Slightly arched, like a pig's back.

Ionic Greek classical order, with scroll decorated capitals.

Jacobean Early 17th century English style, distinguished by striking arrangements of mass and silhouette, and use of mullioned and transomed bay windows.

Jamb Side of a doorway or window.

Lancet Tall, narrow, pointed Gothic window.

Lintel The beam over an opening.

Loggia Covered open arcade.

Lug *Ear-like* projection.

Machicolations Defensive openings in corbelled wall-walk through which missiles might be dropped.

Modillion brackets Flat brackets supporting overhanging eaves or cornice.

Moorish Architectural style of Islamic occupied Spain.

Mullion Upright dividing shaft on window.

Oriel Window projected on corbelling.

Palazzo Italian Renaissance palace, originally with fine apartments above ground floor shops.

Parapet Low wall along the edge of a roof, etc.

Pedestal The support of a column.

Pediment Triangular or circular panel over a window, door, or portico, etc.

Piend Hipped or sloping ended roof.

Pilaster Shallow column projecting from a wall.

Pinnacle Small slender turret or spire.

Portico Colonnade fronting a building.

Quatrefoil Like a four-petalled flower or leaf.

Quoin Dressed corner stone.

Regency Architectural style prevailing 1810-20.

Renaissance Re-birth; the rediscovery of classical architecture in Italy c. 1420, which then spread throughout Europe.

Rib Projecting decorative band on a groin vault.

Romanesque (or Norman) Pre-Gothic style of mediaeval architecture characterised by round-headed arches.

Roundel Round open turret.

Rubble Undressed irregular masonry.

Rustication Stonework where regular blocks are roughened and the joints deeply recessed.

Rybat A dressed stone at the side of a door or window.

Scourge Whip.

Scrolled Ornamented with carved coils.

Segmented Broken into segments of a circle.

Skew Raised coping at the head of a gable.

Skewputt Lowest stone of the skew, often decorated.

Skirting Slate lower courses in a pantile roof to effect a sealed junction of the eaves.

Statute Labour Road Road maintained by compulsory labour.

String course Projecting moulded horizontal course along the face of a building.

Tirlace gate Turnstile, or tollgate.

Tracery Ornamental open-work in the head of a Gothic window.

Transome Horizontal dividing shaft in a window.

Trefoil Three-lobed ornamental form.

Tripartite Window divided vertically in three.

Tudor Late Gothic *Perpendicular* architectural style which pervailed in the 16th century, characterised by English mediaeval castles.

Turnpike Road Toll road, built by the county commissioners following the 18th century *Turnpike Acts.*

Turnpike Stair Narrow spiral staircase.

Tuscan Heavy plain Roman equivalent of the Greek Doric order.

Vault Arched ceiling of stone or brick.

Wedder Sheep Form of *wether,* a castrated ram.